PRAISE FOR
ANSWER THE CALL

As mayor of Sioux City, Iowa, I often brag about the giving nature of the people of our city. Their caring attitude was once again shown when we had the opportunity to host the kids from Tanzania. The Tanzanian kids won the hearts of our citizens and our citizens were blessed by their presence in our community.

I personally had the chance to interact with them four times and every time they had smiles on their faces. I often think about how spoiled we are in this country and I am sure most Americans would not have been as joyful under the same circumstances.

I am so thankful that these kids from Tanzania came to our community and had such an impact on our citizens.

Bob Scott
Mayor of Sioux City

The story of the Miracle Kids is truly incredible. It is the story you will read in Dr. Steve Meyer's book. I have met these three children whose lives so nearly ended in tragedy, and I have met "Dr. Steve," whom I think of as the "Miracle Doctor," who saved them. It was a very moving experience. And when you read this book you will be moved as well. It shows that miracles do, indeed, happen.

Jane Goodall, PhD, DBE
Founder – the Jane Goodall Institute & UN Messenger of Peace

Answer The Call is a message for all of us regarding faith, human kindness, and community.

We should never forget that God has plans for all of us. We often get confused and frustrated with the details on how we will achieve these plans because they are not easy to comprehend. Always remember that faith and human kindness are tools to achieve our plans.

This book and its message truly make me proud to be a Christian, husband, and father. It reminds us that through faith in God any details—big or small—will work themselves out.

Jeremie Davis
Technology Executive – Del Monte, Dannon, Conagra
Current Managing Partner – Ahatis

Being intimately involved in the miracle kids story has transformed my life and given me a whole new perspective on miracles. Reading this amazing story will do the same thing for you.

Steve King
14-year Congressman – Iowa 4th District

My work with medical missions began also in 1994, and I have seen the profound effect on people of unconditional giving. This is the penultimate story of the goodness of people multiplied by being touched by God. Its joy will lift your heart to new levels.

Lawrence D. Dorr, M.D.
Founder – Operation Walk

ANSWER THE CALL

DR. STEVEN MEYER

ON BEHALF OF STEMM & THE COMMUNITY OF SIOUX CITY

ANSWER THE CALL

THE STORY OF THE
MIRACLE KIDS IN TANZANIA

THRONE
PUBLISHING GROUP

Cover Design: Caitlin Pisha
Lead Writer: Angela Tewalt
Editor: Cameron Brooks
Proofing Editor and Publishing Manager: Amy Rollinger

Throne Publishing Group
2329 N Career Ave #215
Sioux Falls, SD 57107
ThronePG.com

DEDICATION

Donald Julius Meyer
10-16-27 to 4-4-18

I strongly need to dedicate this book to my dear dad who passed to be with his Heavenly Father. He was a loving, gifted, and incredibly outgoing man of great character and a strong personal faith. He had an incredibly unique ability to talk to anyone, and at the end of every encounter left you feeling gifted by the conversation.

Possessing only a high school education but with an IQ of 150, he was the smartest man I ever met. His dedication to family, faith and friends model for me everyday the man I am and aspire to be an amazing communicator, he regaled all of his three children and each of his dozen grandchildren with amazing bedtime stories when he would tuck them into bed at night.

A humble man, one of his proudest achievements was having one of those stories published in a magazine. I can only pray to achieve a small portion of the gift of communication and encouragement that he passed on to all of us.

It is for that reason, and the fact that my father modeled in every respect what a good, good Father in Heaven we have, that I dedicate this book to his amazing life and his memory.

TABLE OF CONTENTS

TABLE OF CONTENTS

PART THREE: HOMECOMING

ACKNOWLEDGMENTS

I can do no other than to begin and end with all thanks and glory to my Lord and Savior, Jesus Christ. Beyond that this story was so deep, so wide, and so urgent that I hesitate writing acknowledgments, assured that many persons integral to the wonder of this miracle will be forgotten. To those individuals and groups, I apologize in advance.

My greatest thanks go to incredible men of faith, Congressman Steve King and Reverend Franklin Graham, without whom this entire story would have been impossible. To Samaritan's Purse and especially Drew Privette and Ed Morrow: I have insufficient words to express our gratitude. Their entire team gave joyfully and tirelessly—from pilots to ground crew and office personnel. They not only provided transport both ways for the children, but they provided

ACKNOWLEDGMENTS

38,000 pounds of medical supplies (over $300,000) to local hospitals in Tanzania. They are an amazing team of faithful servants led by a true God Warrior, Franklin Graham.

Dr. Larry Volz and especially Dr. Steven Joyce were amazing in their tireless medical support of the children. Mercy Medical Center—from top administrators Jim Fitzpatrick and Dave Snetter to the sanitation staff—was incredible in their love and support. The time, treasure, and talent freely given by Mercy Medical Center of Sioux City is incalculable.

My partners at CNOS, particularly Doctors Kensinger and Durwood, as well as our entire organization, could not have been more supportive. Thank you!

Bob Scott, our mayor, and Chris McGowan, Chamber President were beyond stellar in leading our entire community in an outpouring of love and encouragement. The magnanimous love and encouragement of our entire community of Siouxland cannot be sufficiently recognized. It was amazing to witness!

The orthopedic and spinal implant company Synthes/ Johnson & Johnson are to be commended for the tens of thousands of dollars of free implants and devices enabling the children's recovery.

The time, love, and resources dedicated by Christy Batien and the Ronald McDonald House in caring for the Miracle Kids and their mothers were incredible. The Ronald

ACKNOWLEDGMENTS

McDonald House became home to all eight Tanzanians a world away from their families.

During her convalescence and miraculous recovery from paralysis, precious Doreen rehabilitated at Madonna Rehabilitation Center in Lincoln, Nebraska. They were a true miracle to Doreen as was the support of Dr. Doug Tewes, his wife Denise, and the congregation of Messiah Lutheran Church.

Pastor Jeff Moss and the entire staff and congregation at Sunnybrook Church embraced the children, their families, Dr. Elias, and Nurse Symphorosa in Christian love and encouragement. They will always consider Sunnybrook their church home away from home.

I cannot fail to mention the phenomenal efforts made by the governments of both the U.S. and Tanzania. In a true example of multinational diplomacy, the U.S. State Department and Embassy were essential in completing this miracle mission. And of course, without Vice President Samia Suhulu and then MP Lazaro Nyalandu this incredible tale would not have happened.

I am so incredibly proud of the entire team at STEMM. From the moment Jennifer, Manda and Kevin insisted the safari truck stop—hurling themselves into the horrific scene of the crash—all three of them have been nothing short of heroic. Their bravery and faith represent the epitome of answering the call. Without them, there literally is no Miracle Kids story to tell. Throughout the rescue, recovery and return of the Miracle Kids, our executive director Jon Gerdts and our entire STEMM team answered the call at every turn, modeling our mission to provide compassionate Christian care!

This incredible tale of love and miracles was instituted by the miracle love of my life, my wife Dana. Without her incredible faith in me and our Savior none of this would have been remotely possible. She and my family are my strength, my ballast and my motivation in life!

And of course all of the innumerable players in this beautiful story owe their very breath and life to our loving Almighty Creator God. He is so good! Thank you, Father!

INTRODUCTION

God is so good.

Life isn't always easy, but there is always triumph in tragedy! (Rom 8:28) This story isn't easy to believe. In fact, it's beyond my comprehension. But this is a true and epic tale of profound joy, immeasurable victory, and Almighty God's eternal presence in our lives.

In this story, and ultimately in life, our loving Father always prevails.

Wherever you are in your journey, He has a plan for you (Jer 29:11). A script for your entire life has already been written, and your purpose awaits. We spend so much of our lives avoiding pain. We gravitate toward routine and avert chaos as much as we can, because that feels safe and in control. However, when we do this, we miss the thrill of seeing God come through. We miss out on God's glory, *His control* and His divine plan. For you.

We have a nonlinear God. His grand design for you is like the back of a needlepoint, chaotic and confusing and frustrating, indeed. But when the tapestry is finished, and you turn the needlepoint around to see it all come together, it's a beautiful masterpiece.

In the end, your life is that same kind of masterpiece, created just for you! Don't you want to be a part of that unique experience in fulfilling your role for God's Kingdom? No one else can be you. No one but YOU can do what God has ordained you to do. You are not irrelevant in His Kingdom! Rather, you are highly relevant and cherished by God, so much that He sent His only Son to die for you and His Holy Spirit to work in *your* heart.

What you have to do is remarkably elementary. Just say YES!

This book is about a lot of yeses. To get to where we are today, many of us had to say YES to many small things—even when we didn't want to—and we had to give God room to show up in a big way.

He did. He continues to today. You'll see.

Unfortunately, we have so much noise in our lives these days that it's challenging to make time for our Father and to invite Him into our hearts. Saying YES has become more and more difficult. We have also become so self-reliant and narcissistic that we don't even want to accept the Spirit trying to work within us—we want to be in control, remember? I understand that more than anyone. Even as I tell this story today, I am still a sinner in need of God's grace. But that doesn't stop me from talking with Him, listening for my calling and obeying His plan for me. I try every day, and you are given that choice, too. Don't be afraid to fail. Our loving Father looks to the heart of what we do. He honors effort and intention, not success. The greatest misstep in His Kingdom is sitting still.

Despite egos and pride, we all have a tremendous hunger to connect and to be a part of the eternal story. But that satisfaction is only met if we choose to serve Him first. Only then can our role take effect.

Regardless of your role, you are not an observer. You are an active participant in God's story, and He loves you so profoundly and wants you to make a difference in His Kingdom. He wants you to shine.

Invite the fear, embrace the chaos, and trust completely in Him.

In this story, three beautiful children affect the hearts and lives of an entire nation, and as you read, you will discover that their journey is beyond evidential that God has a plan indeed. He had a purpose for everything that happened, and even as it seemed impossible, God kept prevailing. I'm humbled to share this incredible story with you.

My prayer is for you to feel empowered, challenged, and CHOSEN. I hope that you renounce any skepticism in your heart and instead embrace the possibility of complete transformation. If God can positively transform a struggling nation through heartbreaking tragedy, He can surely stir enough in your heart to believe in His will.

He desperately desires to get your attention, and I hope this does. Do not be overwhelmed. Take heed, but know that this story and God's work is not bigger than you. God's power is accessible to all, any time, every day. Right now.

With man, it's impossible, but with God, *all things* are possible. Most certainly, a transformation within you.

To our great and loving Father, this glory is all for You.

PART ONE

THE TRAGEDY

CHAPTER ONE

THE FACILITATOR

I am not perfect. In fact, I often question why God chose me, of all people, to be involved in and tell this story. But God does not seek perfection. He seeks a willingness to serve, and that I have shown Him.

But I wasn't always so willing.

I grew up on a small farm in Iowa, and I had loving, encouraging parents. Education was very important to them—it mattered above all else—and they would always tell me, "You can, and you will." I was a bright student and remember telling my fifth-grade teachers that I wanted to be a doctor someday, but they laughed at me. That didn't matter. In fact, it just motivated me all the more. I just kept telling myself, "I can do this."

And I did.

I grew up in a very conservative Lutheran church, but I never really understood the meaning of having a personal relationship with Jesus Christ. God was a magical vending machine in the sky you prayed to when things got bad. The concept was to try to tap into His power when all else failed, and I needed Him. The concept of God wanting to use me was unimaginable.

I went on to college and received a medical degree from the University of Iowa. By then, the more success I had, the less I needed God. God offers much to the poor and demands much of the rich. But I became so rich in myself, I didn't think I needed God.

I certainly could not imagine that God needed me.

I got married while I was in medical school and did a year of family practice residency in Sioux Falls, South Dakota. But that wasn't glamorous enough for me, so I tried to get into orthopedics and failed. To enhance my resume, I then worked for free in the Orthopedic department biomechanics lab in Iowa City for an entire year. To make ends meet—in addition to sixty hours a week in the lab—I moonlighted three twelve-hour shifts in local emergency rooms. I was driven by *my* dream! By God's providence, after that arduous year, I was accepted into the Orthopedic residency program at the University of Kentucky.

During my time in Kentucky, I got divorced and remarried an anesthesiologist, a charming Southern Belle whom everyone adored. We moved to Sioux City, Iowa, and I truly thought *I had made it.* I was living the dream! The only problem was that it was *my* self-centered, narcissistic dream.

A year into our move, my new bride wanted to have a baby. And I did, too! When I was twelve years old, I remember having a vision that God would give me a son—not any son, but one who would be chosen for great things in God's kingdom. But after three years of multiple in vitro procedures, a miscarriage, and adopting a baby—our precious daughter, Alexandra—my wife was in the the midst of a severe psychological crisis. I got to the point where I couldn't tolerate the daily suffering or the overwhelming feeling of failure, and I had an affair with a woman named Dana. When that became public—and my "perfect" reputation went out the window—I became suicidally depressed. *How could I do this to my wife and my image?*

To this day, I vividly remember loading my 12-gauge and being perplexed at how to hold the thirty-inch barrel to my head and still pull the trigger. I had reached the bottom! Only the thought of my mother's grief kept me from pulling the trigger that night.

I had obviously been kicked out of my own house and had found my own apartment. A week after my futile suicidal gesture, Mercy Medical Center calls me at two in the morning. "Dr. Meyer, we know you're not on call, but we've got a gal with a broken leg and the guy on call won't answer his beeper (which never happens, by the way). But this girl is in a lot of pain, and we know you got kicked out of your house and are now by yourself, so would you come take care of her?"

I really did need to get out of that apartment.

Her name was Donna Thomas. She was a nineteen-year-old missionary with the nonprofit organization Youth With A Mission. She was traveling from Arkansas to Michigan to do a youth camp for a year. During an overnight stay in Laurel, Neb., she fell from a trampoline and shattered her tibia, and I was compelled by her story. So after I put a steel rod in her leg, I sat by her bedside and said to her, "It's very impressive that a nineteen-year-old would give her life to God in that big of a way."

Then, I went on to tell her that I was lost and even though I went to church, I was in the middle of a terrible situation and I couldn't find God. She looked me right in the eye and replied, "God didn't move. You did."

As you can imagine, that hit me hard. She was discharged on a Friday, and by that following Tuesday, I got a call with a heavy Southern accent on the other end. "Dr. Meyer, my name is Ann. I'm from Arkansas, and we got a trip planned to China in Juuu-ly, and you're coming along." I replied, "What?

This is a bad accent, which one of my buddies is playing a joke on me!" But it wasn't a joke. "We are a medical team with a trip planned to China," she went on, "but we are really smuggling Bibles from Hong Kong into the mainland, which is a capital offense, but we got the Lord's protection, and anyway, we can't get in without a doctor leading our team. We've got eleven other people, and the Chinese government is going to cancel our visas if we don't get a doctor!"

She continued, "When Donna Thomas walked into my office after getting back from Sioux City, she uttered your name, and the peace of the Holy Spirit came upon me and told me, 'Dr. Meyer is your doctor.'"

I said, "Ann, *you are out of your mind.* There is no way on God's earth I am going with you to China." And I hung up the phone.

But three months later, I went with her to China, and my life forever changed.

I guess she was pretty persistent. The "Hound of Heaven" was calling.

THE BEGINNING OF STEMM

We went to China in the summer of 1995. We smuggled the Bibles quite precariously and nearly got caught. But the second week we were there, we went to an open air church in Hong Kong during a monsoon rain, where a fiery Korean, British-speaking pastor was preaching. He was so charismatic that halfway through the sermon, I fell to my knees in a mud puddle. To be honest, I felt the very hand of God on my neck pushing me to bow down. God clearly spoke to me and said, "I created you for a purpose. I love you enough to give you free will, but I'm calling on you right now. You can either live for yourself, or you can live for me. But you must choose. Now is your time."

And right there in the mud, I accepted Christ into my heart.

When I got back to Sioux City, I told my pastor Jon Gerdts what had happened. I told him I was convicted that God wanted me to get into medical mission work. To that, he responded, "What do you think of Tanzania?"

As it turns out, I thought very highly of Tanzania. I had never been there, but ever since I was a boy, I had been enthralled with Africa. When my incredibly frugal dad splurged and bought the *Encyclopedia Britannica*, I wore out volume A reading all about Africa as a kid. God had put Africa on my heart *for a long time*. It just so happened that Pastor Jon had spent a year in Tanzania after seminary, and he had been praying about an avenue to go back for a mission trip.

Specifically, he had been praying for someone to help lead a mission trip there. I guess that person was me!

So the following summer, a group of twelve of us traveled for the first time to Tanzania—and among that group was Dana. Amid this poignant time in our life, she, too, found God. We reunited, and she joined us on the trip to Tanzania. Moreover, I proposed to Dana while we were there, and we've now been married for twenty years with three beautiful children, all of whom are deeply involved in our ministry today.

God sure does work in mysterious ways, doesn't He? Even in the most blatant, sinful circumstances, if people repent, good things *can* happen. By God's amazing grace, it certainly has for us.

It was a wonderful trip. I'll never forget the moment I walked off the plane at Kilimanjaro International Airport. It was the most overwhelming feeling! I felt like God had poured warm water all over my body, and I was drenched with a feeling of the Holy Spirit.

I was answering my call. I was home.

During our time there, we went to a youth revival, we sang and we prayed, and we also met the First Lady of Tanzania. She challenged us to start a small organization that would help send Tanzanian kids to school. We felt compelled by the idea. When Dana, Pastor Jon, Mike Boose, and I got back to Sioux City, we considered starting a nonprofit and calling it STEMM, Siouxland Tanzania Educational Medical Ministries.

The first time I talked about STEMM was on a Sunday morning TV show. I kept thinking, *who on earth is watching this at 8:30 on a Sunday morning?* Nonetheless, I discussed how we wanted to start an organization that would help Tanzanian children get into secondary school, but that we needed some help. We invited anyone who was interested to come to our house for an informational meeting.

I really didn't think anyone would show up. I remember Dana asking how many cookies she should bake for refreshments. I told her, "Oh, a dozen would easily cover it." But, the following Tuesday, forty-six people drove out to our house, and STEMM commenced. We had "laid out the fleece" and God responded in an overwhelming way! He had answered our prayers and STEMM was born.

When STEMM began in 1997, we started off by sending fifty kids a year to school. To date, we have sent over 10,000 Tanzanian students to secondary school and University—and we have been named the second-best orphanage in all northern Tanzania. We have dug wells, built bridges, and performed over 1,000 operations within our medical ministry. We run a school feeding program for over 2,000 children daily and are committed to community development, especially through agricultural training. Our mission is to change lives for Christ through compassionate care, and our vision is to develop Tanzania into a vibrant Christian community.

With over seventy-five trips to Tanzania—forty-five personally—we have developed a relational bridge between Siouxland and Tanzania by addressing spiritual growth, medical care, community empowerment, and education. We believe the Holy Spirit changes lives by revealing Jesus Christ to us and through us. We are committed to following the great commandment to "Love God above all others" and "Love our neighbors as ourselves." We believe in the transformative power of the Holy Spirit in lives submitted to Jesus Christ.

The past twenty years have been an incredible journey, and we thought we *already* had a great story.

Until we met the Miracle Kids.

THE TRIP

In the spring of 2017, STEMM had planned a trip to Tanzania to celebrate our mission's twentieth anniversary. Even though we hadn't planned on it being a medical trip, I had been considering opening an outreach orthopedic clinic in a remote area called Singida, in the near future. But, when a man named Lazaro Nyalandu called me six weeks before we were to leave, insisting that the Singida clinic needed to happen *now*, I had to scramble for a medical team.

I met Lazaro twenty years ago during my first trip to Tanzania in 1996. He was along when I met the First Lady and they encouraged me to begin STEMM. So not only is Lazaro a former member of the Tanzanian parliament, he was also a co-founder of STEMM and was previously the president of the board in Tanzania. He is a dear friend, an ongoing adviser in our ministry, and an important role in this story.

The first person I ask to join my medical team for this trip was Kevin Negaard. Kevin is the executive director of Sunnybrook, a fast-growing megachurch in Sioux City, Iowa, and has been a close friend for twenty years. He is also an athletic trainer, who at the time was coaching baseball at Morningside College as well as Miracle League. I admit, he was a busy guy, so it is no surprise that he turned me down when I first asked him. But I felt compelled to try harder. I called Jeff, his pastor and boss at Sunnybrook, and told him, "Kevin needs to go on this trip!" A week later, Kevin calls me, clearly bothered. "I was told I'm going to Tanzania, huh?" Drastic times sometimes require drastic measures.

The second member of our medical team was Jennifer Hadley, a nurse practitioner from Dunes Surgical Hospital in Iowa. Five years ago, she hosted a man named Charles, an obstetrician from Tanzania whom I brought to Sioux City for a back operation. She cared for him at her home while he recovered, and since then, she'd been wanting to make a trip with us but could never find the time. I reached out to her and, to my surprise, this time was a yes. She responded immediately, "Yeah, I think I need to go! But you need to talk to my boss to get the time off." Since her boss works for me, that was a no-brainer. Jennifer was in!

Our third and final member of the medical team was Manda Volkers, a nurse who lives in Ponca, Nebraska with her family. In the same week I had asked Kevin and Jennifer to join me, Manda walks into my office with her son, one of my patients. She told me that I operated on her husband fifteen years ago and says, "We love following along with what you do at STEMM!" So I didn't hesitate. I asked her, "Well, do you want to go to Tanzania with STEMM in six weeks?"

And, *she said yes.*

In hindsight, this is a miracle. Six weeks is an epically short time to prepare for a trip for Tanzania, let alone find three medical volunteers who had no intention to make the journey prior to my pleas. But come end of April, we were off to Tanzania.

We visited the orthopedic clinic in Singida on Thursday, May 4. However, within the four months since I had been there last, the government had fired medical personnel, and we walked into an entirely different clinic *that wasn't even expecting us.* We had planned on doing clinic and surgery for up to fifty patients, and we only saw *three*. The medical team I had convinced to drop everything and come to Tanzania suddenly had nothing to do. I was bummed! But Kevin, Jennifer, and Manda were gracious and happy to be with us in Tanzania.

And anyway, God had other plans for them.

CHAPTER TWO

THE CRASH

SATURDAY, MAY 6, 2017

The morning dawned, bleak and gloomy. Rain of the past few days had given way to a steady mist, and clouds loomed low on the East African horizon. But the dreary skies could not dampen the enthusiasm of two very disparate groups of travelers that day. Both groups were about to embark on an exciting day of adventure.

One group was twelve- and thirteen-year-old African children of Lucky Vincent Primary School, who were taking a rare field trip outing. The other was our STEMM team of missionaries. Because the Singida clinic was no longer happening, our group was anticipating a glorious one-day safari in the Ngorongoro District. Little did they know that

God's providence was about to steer them toward a cataclysmic encounter that would change their lives and impact an entire nation.

Wherever God has planted us, life can be difficult, but life as a child in East Africa is particularly challenging. There often is not enough to eat, school attendance is a privilege, and disease and even death are a constant specter, which creates a harsh environment to grow up in, to say the least. Like all East African grade-school children, those of Lucky Vincent Primary School in Arusha struggle with the rigors of daily life.

But comparatively, they are privileged with the opportunity to attend an exemplary private primary (grade) school. They know that their only opportunity to break free from poverty and into productivity is their education. They work diligently and are serious, studious children. There is little time for play, as their future depends on their performance.

But on this Saturday, they were going on a field trip. In Tanzania, students have to take a national exam at the end of eighth grade to qualify for secondary school—or high school, as it's considered in the States. The exam was coming up, so these students were all getting together for a practice test as well as a fun day together. They were going to play soccer and enjoy camaraderie toward the end of the school year. An hour away, an equally excited group was preparing for a day of fun and relaxation. Kevin, Jennifer and Manda—along with two

STEMM board members, the wife of a board member, and a STEMM newcomer from California—were excited for their safari. The Friday night before, I was telling them, "Get to bed early!" They needed to be on the road by 7 a.m. if they wanted to make the safari on time. I told them it was imperative to arrive to the Crater before the animals went to bed.

And, they were late. First, they were forty-five minutes late leaving the lodge, then another fifteen minutes late because they stopped at a scenic outlook and got caught with the street vendors.

They joked about being on slow "African time," but they were surely on God's watch that morning. God had them in His plan.

As soon as they got back on the road, they came upon an accident. They were coming around a corner and down a hill on the Arusha-Manyara Road, near Rotia Village, when they happened upon a massive group of villagers alongside the road, and even more people standing down a deep ravine.

It was a chaos they couldn't ignore.

Jennifer immediately says to the driver, "We have to stop." The driver hesitated. So she says to him again, "No! *You have to stop.*"

As all of our STEMM members got out of their truck, they were introduced to the worst school bus crash in Tanzanian history. The school bus was filled with thirty-five of Lucky Vincent's seventh- and eighth-graders, two teachers, and a bus driver, traveling from Arusha to a sister school near Karatu to perform their mock exams.

It was supposed to be a fun day. *It was supposed to be a special day*. But the roads were wet, and the school bus slid.

It is believed that the driver braked suddenly. As he did, the school bus spun 180 degrees, went airborne, and then nosedived deep into a ravine, instantly killing almost all of the students on board, as well as the teachers and the driver.

As they got out of their truck, Kevin, Jennifer, and Manda immediately ran to the scene. Calmly, their medical instincts kicked in, and their hands went to work.

When they arrived, a few students had already been pulled from the bus, so the three of them began triaging. Even though there were broken bones and severed limbs at the scene, they were checking pulses before even evaluating bone fractures.

They were listening for hearts.

Kevin says, "*I remember checking kids over and over to make sure I wasn't wrong. I would straighten out the gross deformities of the dead, close their eyes and make them look as dignified as possible. Most every kid had bilateral wrist fractures from putting their hands up to brace themselves. That bus came to a sudden stop with such force. There was plenty of bad, open and closed fractures and limbs broken and sticking in every direction, but there was not a lot of blood.*"

At the scene, people continued to gather, and it was getting louder and louder. No one spoke English, but they did not interfere with Kevin, Jennifer, and Manda's work. Instead, the locals formed a chain from the accident scene up to the top of the ravine, as it was very steep, slippery, and muddy. So they would hand off bodies from the bus and up toward Kevin, Jennifer, and Manda, where each body could be safely triaged and cared for as needed.

Of the thirty-eight victims, only five were at the scene with a remaining heartbeat. Then, a van of locals arrived at the scene to help transport the surviving victims to Mt. Meru Regional Hospital. There were no backboards or stretchers, so it was all they could do to lay the victims carefully in the van and get them to medical attention. Kevin notice later that, when medical personnel finally arrived, only then did they use their stretchers on the already-dead bodies to carry to a police car, where they were piling in all the bodies.

It was an eerie and devastating scene in the middle of Tanzania, a world away from home.

As soon as medical personnel arrived, our rescuers left the scene. Without a word, they simply waved that they were leaving and walked solemnly back to their truck. They washed their hands with wipes and hand sanitizers, and they said a prayer.

Kevin says, "*I remember thinking the kids were so young and gone, just like that. I had a thought of 'those poor parents' who sent their kids off to school, and they would never return home again.*"

They spent that day in a grieving shock. They decided to continue on with their safari, because what more could they have done? The day did serve as a reprieve, and Kevin said while on the safari, they saw the most beautiful, spectacular rainbow stretch across the sky, a sure sign that God was with them that day, guiding them exactly where their hands and help needed to be.

A world away from home, but right where they needed to be.

That evening, they showered, had drinks, and finally began to talk about the accident. Their hearts ached for the survivors. Would they make it? While at the scene of the accident, they didn't even know where the kids were being sent and didn't think they would have any way of seeing them again. And so they went to sleep, praying for peace.

SUNDAY, MAY 7, 2017

On Sunday morning, the remainder of our team drove to Arusha to attend an English-speaking church, and that's when I met up with Kevin, Jennifer, and Manda for the first time since the crash. Their hearts were clearly heavy, and our church service brought upon them even more emotion. Already, God was stirring in me. Clearly, He had been stirring in all of us.

After church, I had business meetings to tend to, so Kevin, Jen, and Manda went souvenir shopping at the Maasai Alley shops in downtown Arusha—an afternoon of mindless shopping to ease the heartache.

While the other were shopping, Kevin was sitting with their driver when he noticed a shop owner reading a newspaper. He asked his driver, Rickey, to go see if there was any news about the bus crash or any survivors.

There was, of course. This event had rocked the nation.

As Rickey brought the paper back to him, Kevin saw a picture of *himself* on the cover of the newspaper, along with the news that there were *three survivors*, and they were in a hospital only five minutes away. Of course, they wanted to go to them immediately!

They were exhilarated, but there was a problem. At this time, it was 6:15 p.m., and the hospital closed at 6. They were told there was absolutely no way to see the kids. No visitors were allowed, not even the rescuers. But while they were standing in the parking lot, a group of well-dressed African men and women approached them immediately and stated,

"You were the Americans at the accident who saved the kids." And they replied, "Yes, we are! Can you take us to them?" It was Tanzania's Permanent Secretary of Health, and he took them to the ICU.

There they met Sadhia, Wilson, and Doreen. They met our Miracle Kids.

At the scene of the accident, Wilson was the only victim who was still conscious. He spoke good English to Jen and Manda, but he had a huge head injury and an obvious humerus bone fracture on both arms. Sadhia's eyes were open at the scene, but they were fixed and dilated, and she was unresponsive. She also had a severe neck injury, and Kevin, Jen, and Manda didn't expect her to survive. Doreen was unconscious at the scene and had a severe open-jaw fracture. Among the three of them, they had well over twenty fractures.

Kevin says, "*When we got into the ICU, we first saw Doreen, who was conscious but could not speak because of her fractured jaw. She had very expressive eyes, and that is how we communicated with her. She also had four fractured vertebrae in her back as well as terrible hip, knee, and arm fractures. She was the most seriously injured. Then we saw Sadhia, the girl we thought we would never see alive again! She was unconscious, but they said she had been responsive during the day. And then Wilson, hand stitched up but aware and talking with us, and sharing huge smiles with us. That moment was very healing for Jen, Manda, and me. I think it was assuring that maybe we did make a difference."*

But the circumstances at the hospital were dire. There were no monitoring devices, no available equipment to be seen, no ventilating machines, and very few IV bags. The ICU was incredibly under-resourced, leaving Kevin, Jen, and Manda to feel tremendous unrest. If anything, seeing these three children alive, but under such inadequate care, left them feeling even more heartache. But the doctors and nurses shared freely with them and were thankful for their rescue. And most of all, all three kids were tough, brave, and resilient. But there was no doubt they needed a miracle for their very survival.

After visiting the kids at Mt. Meru Regional Hospital, Kevin, Jen, and Manda returned to our STEMM orphanage late Sunday night where they had internet and were finally able to connect with their families via cell phone. It was a moment of heartache and healing.

At this time, I was out on the veranda alone—doing my Bible study—while the rest of the STEMM team was meeting and talking with one another inside. I needed time alone with God to personally assimilate all this chaos. Then my wife, Dana, texts me.

Mind you, she's one hundred feet away! But instead of to ask me face to face, she texts this: "We need to bring those kids back to America."

Now, my first text back to her is, "*ARE YOU KIDDING. YOU MUST BE CRAZY.*" But she says, "We've been thinking and praying about it over here, and God wants us to bring the three survivors back to America!" At that moment, I start to text back, "This is impossible ..." Think of it! What hospital in the States is going to take in severely injured Tanzanian children? It would be hundreds of thousands of dollars in medical care, all free. And how would we get them passports and visas in time when they needed proper care *now*? Above all, there was no way the sovereign Tanzanian government would agree to let Americans help their own children.

Then I kept thinking ... Even if they would say yes, and even if I did find an American hospital to agree to free medical care, how could we transport three critically injured Tanzanians to the States? In my mind, it was one in a thousand odds for each of these three independent factors, which is one in a billion odds! This was a moon shot! I remember saying to God, "That literally is impossible." So what did I do?

I said yes. Somehow, the passage, "With man, it is impossible, but all things are possible with God," popped into my head at that very moment.

Somehow, I have no idea, I stopped myself from an adamant no and thought, *God, we are your servants in this.* So I suspended my disbelief in that moment and responded to my wife, "If God wants it to happen, I'll do what I can."

It was a thread in my needlepoint. Small yeses lead to big results. God was stirring in some mighty ways.

The first person I call is Lazaro. He already knew of the accident, so when I call, I say, "Dana thinks we need to take these kids to America. Is there any way we can make that happen?" He asked if I was crazy, but then responds, "Let's go for it."

Another small yes.

Then I call Iowa congressman Steve King. He's a good friend. I call him around 9 p.m. that Sunday night. I'm in Tanzania, and he's in Albania for congressional delegation, yet somehow he answers my call. I explain the story, and his response? "This sounds impossible, but I'll do what I can. You can count on me."

Another small yes.

Lastly, so late at night, I call Dr. Steven Joyce, the co-medical director at Mercy Medical Center in Sioux City, Iowa. He doesn't answer, so I leave him a voicemail and tell him about the crash.

At 1 a.m. that night, I go to bed physically, mentally, and spiritually exhausted. What had just happened? Kevin, Jen, and Manda weren't even supposed to be on this trip. Two months ago, Tanzania wasn't even *on their minds*. But suddenly, they had become rescuers, heroes to three beautiful, courageous Tanzanian children. And now I suddenly felt their fate in my hands. On my heart was an aching, I was compelled. I wanted to avoid the pain!

I remember thinking, *there is no way this is going to happen...*

But, God, if this is Your plan, then we have a lot of work to do.

PART TWO

THE MOVEMENT

CHAPTER THREE

THE ANNOUNCEMENT

MONDAY, MAY 8, 2017

At 5 a.m., Lazaro calls me. "Hey, are you up? You gotta be in town in the next hour!"

I guess I was up then. Thanks, brother!

We meet and have coffee, and then he tells me to get in his truck. "We got to meet somebody," he says. He wouldn't tell me who, but soon enough, we drive up to a highly-guarded compound. There was security everywhere! As we walk through the door Lazaro says to me, "Steve, I'd like you to meet Mama Samia Hassan Suluhu, the vice president of Tanzania."

I was wearing jeans. Lazaro introduces me as "Dr. Steve from America."

The first thing she says to me is, "Yes, I remember you as a very nice young man." She was present when I met the First Lady with Lazaro over twenty years ago, and she remembered me!

As I begin to tell her our story and explain to her that we need to get these kids to America, she remains stoic. She nods, and looks me in the eye, but gives me nothing. It was absolutely impossible to tell; was she empathetic? Was she going to help?

Was she going to answer her call the way so many had before her?

She leaves me in complete suspense, but I remember feeling *so* energized. I was afraid to get my hopes up, but I had a good feeling. At least, I was prayerfully hopeful.

From her compound, Lazaro, Mama Suluhu, and I— along with a dozen of her people—drive to the hospital to see the children. This is the first time I see the kids.

This is the first time I meet and begin a whole new life with Sadhia, Doreen, and Wilson.

It is a rainy, drizzly day, just like the morning of the bus crash, and it is ominous. When I meet the kids, they are not well. Wilson had an open femur fracture with a bloody cast on, and both of his arms were broken. Sadhia still wasn't speaking to any of us, and Doreen had a shattered jaw and was in dire pain. I was overjoyed to see them, but there is palpable fear in my heart. How could we ever help these children here? It was obvious to me that they were amid a long and painful demise.

That same morning, the Tanzanian government had sent in a team of doctors from Dar es Salaam, the largest city in Tanzania, to evaluate the care of the kids. They first were trying to convince me that they could take care of them themselves, but I insisted that each of them needed better care in order to survive. And when the minister of health stated that these Miracle Kids were "shining stars of the country and needed to survive," the doctors conceded and agreed to send the kids wherever they needed to go for proper care. It was still a "moon shot," but just hearing that concession from the medical authorities was a relief, one small step toward our dream for these children.

Kevin says, "*Seeing the kids was an inspiration. Sadhia was awake but would not speak to us, and turned away whenever we approached her. She only spoke in Swahili to the nurses. Doreen's face was even more swollen from her broken jaw, and her mom was trying to feed her with a spoon, because, of course, there was no feeding tube at this hospital. Doreen did start writing to me in a little journal I gave her as her form of communication. She wrote about how she saw and remembered the accident, and how she saw her favorite teacher dead. And then she asked me if I knew her friend Ruth, who was from Chicago. I had no idea what she meant at the time, but a doctor later explained to me that Ruth was Doreen's best friend and was killed in the bus crash, and that Ruth had a young lady from Chicago who befriended her and supported her. So when I got back to the States, this supporter had posted on Facebook about the loss of Ruth, and I was able to contact her and share updates about the kids."*

Remember, the vice president of Tanzania is along with us while we are visiting the kids at the hospital. And while we are there, she receives a phone call. As I watch her pick up her phone, I can see the name, "John Magufuli," the president of Tanzania, on the other line.

I gasp.

She excuses herself to the corner of the room, and as she speaks with him, she is nodding and shaking her head seriously. When she returns with a solemn face, she says nothing.

But she had our answer, and God knew. What was it?

MONDAY AFTERNOON

From the hospital, we all drive in a caravan to the memorial. Even though it was only two days since the accident, a massive memorial had already been planned for the thirty-five victims we lost on Saturday.

It was already surprising that we would be attending their memorial, but we were not prepared for what was to come. An entire nation came together to mourn this loss, and it was an unbelievable sight.

The funeral was held at a soccer stadium that seated 15,000, but there were over 100,000 Tanzanians present that day—not to mention the millions who were watching on TV from around the world. BBC and Voice of America were covering the event. There were bleachers around three-fourths of the stadium and a large, covered grandstand where over 30,000 people crowded in. Then, there were another 70,000 guests outside the stadium, just wanting to be near and memorialize the kids. Just to get a glimpse inside, they were climbing onto the back of the stadium and onto roof-tops of nearby buildings. They were sitting in massive trees that hung over the walls of the stadium and hanging outside hotel windows.

None of us had ever seen a sight quite like this.

When we arrived, it was still three hours before the memorial was to begin, but even so, we couldn't get close. I was with Lazaro and ended up being escorted into the covered grandstand, where many dignitaries had already been seated. As for the rest of our STEMM team, they were sitting at the top of the grandstand. We wouldn't see each other until long after the memorial had begun.

In front of the grandstand was a large, white tent and many white tables in a line. This is where the caskets would be placed. On either side of the larger tent were smaller tents for the families. It was a beautiful service—so much respect for these children—but the grief was nearly impossible to bear. I can still hear the wails. They haunt me to this day.

Africans are very demonstrative in their grief. Whatever they are feeling, they welcome it and accept it and take it all in; they do not hold back. Culturally, this outpouring is a necessary response to deal with tragedy—let alone a national tragedy that took the lives of thirty-two innocent children. And with thousands of Tanzanians present that day to mourn these children, the cries and wails and weeping was impossible to bear. How could you not succumb to their grief? It was one of the darkest, saddest scenes I've ever witnessed.

As the memorial begins, massive military trucks start driving into the stadium to unload the caskets onto their white tables. One by one, casket after casket is laid quietly as the audience continue to sob. Nearly every casket has a cross and a picture of the deceased. It was respectful, a grand gesture for these families.

As eulogies begin, everyone is crying—so much so that ambulances are present to take away grieving people. Women are passing out, and stretchers are carrying away fellow students and parents who were convulsing in their heartache. At least one hundred people were taken away that afternoon.

The eulogies go on for over three hours, and all the while, it rains. The skies are gray and dismal, and the grounds are wet and muddy. Everything is cold, dark, heavy, and somber.

Then, the vice president of Tanzania, Mama Suluhu, steps up to speak.

She speaks in Swahili: "Before I say any words to memorialize our dead children, I first must recognize the three American heroes who without, we would have three more caskets here today."

I look up to Kevin, Manda, and Jen in the stands. My heart is breaking for the epic tragedy they embraced. Then, I hear her say, "I especially want to thank Dr. Meyer for his promise to take our children back to America."

Wait. *What?* You can't be serious!

I look to my wife. Her eyes are as big as mine. How bold of Mama Suluhu to not say a word of this all day then wait to announce in front of thousands of her people—and the millions watching on TV no less!—that I would be saving her children. It was the biggest affirmation, but my heart was pounding.

I was terrified. Now the weight of an entire grieving nation was thrust upon my shoulders.

I remember wrestling with the passage from Romans, "God works for the good of those who love Him, who have been called according to His purpose," but what good could come from this? Even though I knew it made sense, even though I knew it needed to happen in order for the kids to survive, bringing them to America suddenly seemed like an insurmountable task. I felt such a heavy sense of responsibility.

Not only was I terrified of failing God and not doing my best, I was terrified of failing an entire country. Tanzania *needed* a ray of light to shine onto this incredible darkness, but how could I provide for them? I had always felt like Tanzania had given my life purpose, but in that moment, I found myself asking, *why me, God?*

I wanted to run away. Maybe I almost did! I felt a desire to close my eyes and pretend that none of it had happened—or that Mama Suluhu had rather said, "And we have incredible experts from Dar es Salaam coming to care for the kids."

Because that's what we do in the face of fear, right? We imagine there is no burden, after all, or we beg for it to disappear. But that's not what she said. My burden was not gone. Instead, she called my name. God put it on her tongue to call to me, and I had to answer that call.

As we all should, I had to face the fear, welcome my inadequacy and the hardship, and act on God's will.

Though the burden was still heavy, there was a steely resolve within me, and I accepted the work. I couldn't yet envision the solution—we just now had confirmation from the Tanzanian government. What hospital in Sioux City would possibly agree to commit hundreds of thousands of dollars to care for three unknown, broken African children? Even if someone would commit to that, how could we possibly transport them 10,000 miles across the Atlantic? But I trusted that God knew how this would end, so I took a deep, deep breath from the dark and balmy air, and I asked for His guidance.

Then, the skies opened up, and it began to rain hard. It pours on us, and chaos ensues. As people from every direction were rushing toward the tents to pay their own respects, masses of others were also trying to exit the stadium to escape the rain. Even as we got out of the stadium, there was mud and masses of people everywhere. Our team was fearful that someone was going to get hurt!

We escape the stadium and meet for lunch. Everyone is soaking wet and muddy, and yet we all look to each other saying, "Can you believe what just happened? Can you believe what she said?!" But right then and there, we ALL committed. I remember saying to them, "You guys pray. I'll get to work!"

And almost immediately, progress begins. While at lunch, I try once again to call Dr. Joyce from Mercy Medical Center in Sioux City, and this time, he answers.

He says to me, "Mercy *is in*. Money is not an issue. We will take the kids." Mercy and Dr. Joyce had answered their call.

In that moment, I prayed, "Lord give me strength, faith, and wisdom."

CHAPTER FOUR

THE CALL

Over the next forty-eight hours, I imagine I made over 500 phone calls to get these kids to the States. I slept maybe an hour during that time. I remember my fingertips were black from scratching all the calling cards, over and over. While I was on one phone call, I was making a list of three other names I could call as soon as I hung up.

It was endless, but we had little time. Our flight back home was to leave on Wednesday night at 8 p.m., and we had to leave the STEMM compound at 5. The vice president had made her announcement on Monday afternoon, so we had just two days to fulfill our promise.

Steve King and Lazaro were instrumental in our success. They were working with three different embassies and helping the Tanzanian government figure out the kids' passports and visas while I was on the phone with Homeland Security, state departments, politicians, and doctors to make all the necessary arrangements. My mind still reels just thinking of the chaos!

TUESDAY, MAY 9, 2017

On Tuesday morning, we visited the kids again and met with their doctors to discuss what would need to be done should we find a way to fly the kids to America. There was pushback once again. But during that time, the Tanzanian government did agree to send the mamas to Dar es Salaam to get passports and visas ready.

Along with Sadhia, Doreen, and Wilson, we had agreed to take their mothers to America as well. The Tanzanian government also asked that a Tanzanian doctor and nurse come along to be there for the kids and to keep in touch with the hospital in Arusha. So along with the Miracle Kids, we would be flying to the States three mothers, Dr. Elias Mashala, and Simphorosa, the nurse who had to bag Doreen for over six hours before she started to breathe on her own because they had no ventilation at the hospital. What a testament to her care under impossible conditions!

Kevin says, "*When we visited the kids on Tuesday morning, Doreen was writing to us to communicate. Wilson was talkative and smiling, and Sadhia was more awake but still not talking to us. Doreen had wonderful family support that we got to meet. Her parents were so sweet to us, even though they could not speak English. When Dr. Meyer talked to the kids about the possibility of going to America, Wilson and Doreen were excited, but Sadhia was always quiet and scared. The pressure and stress was building, as we were scheduled to leave Tanzania on Wednesday. Time was running out!*"

At 7 p.m. on Tuesday night, I received a call from former White House strategist, Steve Bannon's, chief of staff. She says to me, "Stay up all night, because before Steve goes to bed tonight, he's going to call you to hear your story to then present to Mike Pence tomorrow."

That was such good news! That call would potentially be our confirmation from the U.S. government, and I felt confident they would help us. I knew they had fully-equipped military planes that could easily fly to Tanzania to pick up the kids, right?

So, I stay up all night. But by 5 a.m. in Tanzania, I still had not heard from Steve Bannon. I call congressman Steve King in a panic, "The White House was supposed to call me, and they never did." Steve says, "Then, that's your answer. That must mean no." He had received a heads-up that the government said no as soon as they realized the kids were not U.S. citizens.

I was frustrated. It was Wednesday morning, and we needed to be at the airport in twelve hours. We would potentially be leaving these kids with no hope at all. Failure was knocking loudly at the door of my heart.

WEDNESDAY, MAY 10, 2017

Defeated, we all go back to the hospital in the morning to say goodbye to the kids. It was heartbreaking: not only could it be the last time we'd see them, but they most likely would not survive. Particularly the two girls. Charming Wilson at best would end up with an amputation.

Kevin says, "*I had tears in my eyes as we left the hospital, not knowing if I would ever even see the kids again or if they would get the care they needed and deserved. I will never forget the eyes of Doreen's family. They were very thankful for what we had done, but they had this look of, 'Please, please get our daughter to America so she has a chance to live a normal life.'*

"*It was all so emotional. We knew God had a purpose and that our lives would forever be changed by these three kids. But what were God's plans? Why would He bring us here to Tanzania, to the accident site, and then not allow us to get the kids to the U.S. for the care they needed? But I knew He had a plan. I knew His timing was perfect."*

By the time we get back to the STEMM orphanage, it's 4:30 in the afternoon and we need to leave for the airport at 5. Our time was completely running out.

I begin packing up in our guest house when Dana walks in and says to me, "What are you packing for? You're not going anywhere. You cannot leave if we don't get these kids out of here!"

Now, I fully understood her sentiment. Of course, I had already been thinking I needed to stay back to care for the kids myself and to operate on them in Arusha. And, clearly the Tanzanian doctors had already implied as much. But I have family and work back at home! I had surgeries scheduled for the following Monday and patients to tend to there. Do you understand the tumult in my mind? I felt such a grave responsibility for these children—and for their nation—but that sudden responsibility could not trump the life I had back at home. I had made a commitment to God and to Tanzania to do everything I could for them, but my life still called for me, too. It was an absolute heartache.

I say to Dana, "I'm going home." She says to me, "You are not!" And as she rebuttals, she is literally removing my socks and underwear from my duffel bag and throwing them to the ground. What a scene! I sincerely thought fisticuffs with my dear wife was imminent.

In that moment, I felt despair. Had I really failed? Despite what felt like Herculean effort and so much heartfelt prayer, our hopes were on life support. God had moved *mountains*, but a seemingly insurmountable chasm—the Atlantic ocean!—still remained. Had God led us this far to abandon us now?

Then I hear my ringtone.

My phone is out on the patio, so I run to it. As I look down, I see it's a North Carolina number, and my first thought is, *How did a telemarketer find me in Tanzania?* Disgruntled, I answer the phone anyway.

The voice on the other end says, "Dr. Meyer, this is Franklin Graham."

Now, I'm rarely speechless and never breathless, and I was both. *It was Billy Graham's son!*

He continues, "I'm with Samaritan's Purse." (Which is such a cool understatement. He *is* Samaritan's Purse!) He says, "I talked to congressman Steve King, and I want to help you."

As it turns out, Steve King reached out to Franklin Graham, Graham talked to his administrative team, and at the perfect hour, Franklin calls me to say they've agreed to fly the kids to America. Samaritan's Purse is a Christian humanitarian aid organization that provides spiritual and physical aid to hurting people around the world, and they have DC-8 cargo planes that could transport our Miracle Kids all the way from Tanzania to North Carolina, and then by Gulf Stream to Mercy Medical Center in Iowa.

Reverend Graham answered his call in a big way. And his team was less than enthusiastic! Their organization uses DC-8s to fly relief supplies into national disasters, not for medical evacuation. But when one of his staff pointed out that they "don't do that kind of thing," Franklin's response was, "This is exactly what we *should* be doing!"

Once I explained to Mr. Graham that the kids needed to be lying down on the plane and not sitting up, he responded that he would confirm with the FAA and then get back to me as soon as he could.

And we hung up the phone.

Admittedly, that wasn't yet a full YES from Franklin Graham, but it was good enough for me, so I run to the team excitedly and say, "That was Franklin Graham, and Samaritan's Purse is going to try to fly the kids home!"

And then I remember thinking to myself, *"Did I just lie?"* He still had to confirm it. But my heart was confident—*and* that was my way out of the country without having to arm-wrestle my wife!

We were all going home. And hopefully, prayerfully, miraculously, so were the three children.

As we all boarded the plane, everyone was anxious. We kept buzzing, "Samaritan's Purse will come through, right?" It was an eight-hour plane ride to Amsterdam, a welcome reprieve. I was exhausted, but I felt a sense of peace. Yet I also was filled with incredible anxiety at the prospect of one final disappointment.

When we landed in Amsterdam, I could not connect to the internet fast enough. But as soon as I opened my laptop, I saw a message from the CEO of Samaritan's Purse saying, "We are in."

We all just began to weep with joy. We were hugging, praying, and celebrating.

We did it.

Kevin says, "*I boarded the plane at Kilimanjaro International Airport that night emotionally exhausted, thankful for my experience and feeling like I was truly the hands and feet of Jesus. He had me right where he wanted me to be. I was very proud of the work Manda, Jen, and I had done and had felt a strong connection with them. We were three people who did not even know each other ten days prior to the accident. We were all at varying places in our walks with the Lord, yet we were all brought together for that moment. While we were shopping on Sunday, I found a print that had three Massai warriors on them, because to me, it represented us. Three brave, courageous, Massai-like warriors—at least for that hour of our lives.*"

Warriors, rescuers, and heroes who would now get to see those three children get well. From amid death on a deep ravine to harrowing hospital circumstances, our Miracle Kids were finally getting a second chance at life.

CHAPTER FIVE

THE OPERATIONS

At the airport in Tanzania, it was like a celebration. Unlike the mourning crowds who gathered for the memorial, joyous cheers and raucous good-byes swarmed Sadhia, Doreen, and Wilson as they boarded the Samaritan's Purse plane on Sunday morning. Families hugged and kissed, and there were tears of worry, too, as these three children left their homeland. But overall, thousands of Tanzanians were rejoicing for their Miracle Kids.

By God's providence, they were going to survive. At the very least, they were going to be given the best medical care available.

Once Samaritan's Purse had confirmed their commitment, frantic planning spun into motion on both sides of the ocean. The U.S. Embassy processed passports and visas for the children, their mothers, and the doctor and the nurse in forty-eight hours. Six U.S. Embassy staff volunteered on a Saturday, their day off, to make it all happen.

In the States, things were equally frenetic, yet amazingly fruitful. Dr. Joyce, who had advocated for the kids from our first call, was joined by his co-medical executive director, Dr. Larry Volz, in facilitating all of the medical, surgical and emotional care for the kids.

I was taking hourly phone calls with Drew Privette of Samaritan's Purse, who continued to update me on their arrival in the States. At 11 p.m. on Sunday night, he finally called to tell me they had landed in North Carolina. Hallelujah! Paramedics were alerted for transport. Hospital staff were alerted for transport. But even though they were just supposed to switch planes and be on their way to Iowa, *an engine blew*, and they were *grounded*. Unbelievable! That never happens. So close and yet so far. The anticipation here was so heightened! But after a brutal air transport across the Atlantic, these kids needed stabilization quick and were rushed to Carolinas Medical Center in Charlotte, where an ER doctor insisted they stay there to begin surgeries.

He called me frantic at 5 a.m., "They need to stay here."

But I was not about to let a week's worth of work and prayer go out the window.

Donate Today!

Spirit Led - Relationally Driven

Transforming lives through:

- Educational support
- Orphan care
- Medical assistance
- School feeding program
- Cultural tourism
- Agricultural Center of Excellence
- Amputee program
- Community Development/well projects

Text STEMM to 28950

Or visit:

stemm.org

505 5th Street
PO Box 506
Sioux City, IA 51102
Phone: 712-258-8282
E-mail: office@stemm.org

I said to him calmly, "That sounds like a reasonable thought, and I do appreciate the offer, but God wants these kids in Sioux City, so put them on a plane as soon as it's ready."

So on the plane they went.

Doreen was sent to Sioux City first, on her own plane, because her condition was most eminent. By the time she arrived on Monday afternoon, she was paralyzed from the waist down. So they got her checked in and her x-rays completed, and we were operating on her hip by 5 p.m. Then, after her hip surgery—which was the worst hip fracture I have ever seen—a maxillofacial surgeon Dr. Jeff Dean operated on her jaw until after midnight.

She did incredibly well.

Kevin says, "*After they got Doreen into surgery, I went back to the airport to await the arrival of Sadhia and Wilson, who were arriving together on a second plane. When they landed, Sadhia shocked me by actually looking at me and smiling and even talking to me in English. This never happened in Tanzania! But she later told me that I was the first 'mazungo' (white man) she had ever met, and when I bent over her hospital bed to talk to her, I was so close to her that I scared her. That makes complete sense, but I was clueless! Wilson, of course, was big smiles when they landed.*"

Wilson and Sadhia were operated on all day Tuesday. Wilson had an open femur fracture that we put a rod in.

He had an elbow fracture on the left, a humerus fracture on the right, and a forearm fracture that we casted. The big risk for Wilson was his open femur fracture, as it was left open for nine days. But miraculously, he didn't get an infection—none of them suffered any infections during that time. Isn't that unbelievable?

Sadhia was miraculously still alive, despite having fixed and dilated pupils at the scene. She had an odontoid neck fracture at the local hospital in Arusha, where I had to argue with the lead surgeon on whether she had a spine injury. Her shattered arms also were casted and her crushed femur bone was surgically stabilized with a metal rod.

All the kids did so well during all their surgeries, and the mamas were so kind and supportive.

Six days after their arrival, once all of the surgeries had been completed, Congressman King came to visit, along with the Tanzanian ambassador to the U.S. Although Mr. King was the linchpin in the whole story, he had not yet seen the Miracle Kids. He was in awe of Wilson's charisma, charmed by Sadhia's beauty and wit, and mesmerized by Doreen's spirit. After speaking with all three of them, I remember he walked down the hall a few steps in front of Dana and I. I heard him mutter to himself, "This is the most important thing I have ever done," and that came from the mouth of a man who has been a member of congress for fourteen years.

INVITING GOD IN

On Thursday, we took Doreen back into the OR to stabilize her spine. It was a risky and invasive surgery, as we needed to put fourteen screws into her back. I was terrified.

When we operate in Africa, we all put hands on the patients, and we pray aloud before we begin. But in the States, I'm told not to do that, as it's not politically correct, so I usually settle for a silent prayer. But before we began our crucial work on Doreen, I was compelled to call on God. This operation was her only hope for a future, and she needed all the love and prayer we could muster.

One of my dearest friends, colleague and fellow believer, Dr. Quentin Durward, also happens to be a world-class neurosurgeon, and he, too, had answered the call and assisted me on the other side of the operating table during Doreen's surgery. He was a great comfort to me as we were putting screws in her spine that were never meant for someone as small as she was.

I said to everyone in the OR, "If prayer out loud offends anybody, please step out of the room now, because we need to pray." Then, I put my hands on sweet Doreen, and I said, "God, this is your child. You brought her here for a reason, and even though it is not medically feasible, I know you are the God of healing, and I know you are going to restore

Doreen. I am claiming this victory in your Son's name, that Doreen will walk off the airplane when she returns home to Tanzania. I am going to be Your instrument. Guide my hands, God, so she can walk again."

We boldly invited God into that operating room that day. We stated right then, "God, we cannot do this surgery without your presence." And Doreen needed that conviction in us! So often in our lives, we are afraid to declare God's power. We pray with timidity, fearful that He might not hear us, or fearful that He might not listen. I know this to be true, for so many times in my own life, I have shown God my doubt. Just like you, I have been frustrated in disbelief. But in that moment, as I stood above Doreen, her life in my hands, *I felt so empowered*. What I had seen in the last two weeks was beyond belief. I wouldn't believe this story myself if I were reading it right now! But I lived it, I watched our heroes save those children, I fought to keep them alive, and there I stood, answering my call and delivering God's will as He saw it.

In tragedy, there is always triumph. We need to approach the Throne of Grace with boldness, knowing that God is our Loving Father. He has a plan, indeed, and we are His instruments. When we succumb to his script, when we say YES to our Lord, miracles do happen.

Today, Doreen is walking and alive and full of joy. Her abundant life is just one more in a series of miracles within this story that demonstrates how God is working through us and with us and in us.

I am a testament to the universal truth that God uses the most improbable people to do the most impossible things. I wasn't qualified to run this mission, but I surrendered. Somehow, I said YES to my first mission trip to China, I said YES to Tanzania, and then, twenty years later, I said YES to bringing home three beautiful children and giving them a life they deserved. In answering our call, we operated on Doreen, surrendering her fate to God's hands and giving Him all the glory.

With God, all things are possible. I know this to be true.

Late the following Tuesday, I went in to examine Doreen. I asked her, "Can you move?" Nothing. I asked again, touching her toes, "Doreen, can you feel this?" Nothing. I was starting to lose hope. I walked out to dictate her notes, but just as I was finishing, I hear the nurse shout, "Get in here right now! She is wiggling her toes!" And then after I witnessed wiggling of the toes on the left foot, I go back to amend my dictation, then again I hear, "Get back in here! Now she is moving her right leg! She is kicking!"

And I wept. God's will was coming true.

We tell this story today because faith is contagious. It's easy to be afraid or to abandon your belief in God, but if you choose instead to pay attention—to listen to His will and to lean in to the truth—God will reveal Himself in incredible, powerful, unimaginable ways. When people felt and saw my resolve in Doreen's operating room, they folded their hands and prayed to God in their own way, and they started to believe.

You, too, can be bold. Do not be afraid! Your calling awaits.

News footage of the crash.

*The STEMM team rescuers Jennifer, Manda and Kevin
spring into action at the crash scene.*

The horror at the scene.

The land rainbow the day of the crash while on safari.
A sign to us that God was with us in this!

The entire nation of Tanzania grieves the loss of 32 of their children.

Vice President Suhulu paying her respects to the dead children at the memorial service. Moments before she had thanked Dr. Steve for his "promise" to take the kids back to America.

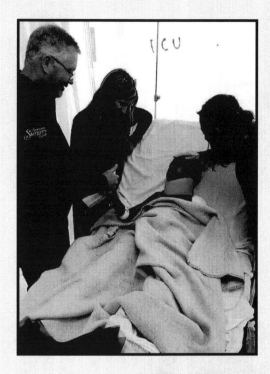

The STEMM rescue team with Doreen at Mt Meru Hospital in Arusha.

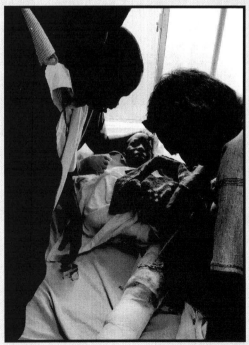

Dr. Meyer prepping Wilson and his cast for transport to America.

Doreen arrives in Sioux City in highly critical condition.

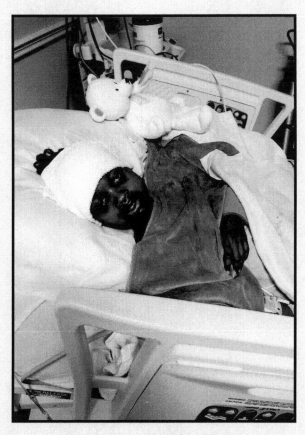

Doreen after life changing surgery by
maxillofacial surgeon, Dr. Jeff Dean.

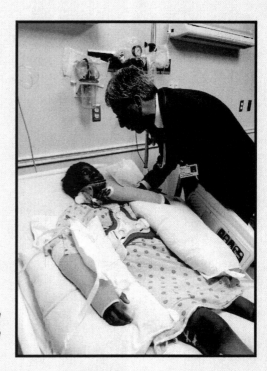

Dr. Joyce with Sadhia. She calls him her Tanzanian father.

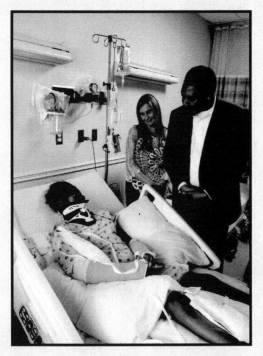

The Tanzania Ambassador made a visit to Mercy Medical Center in Sioux City to see the Miracle Kids.

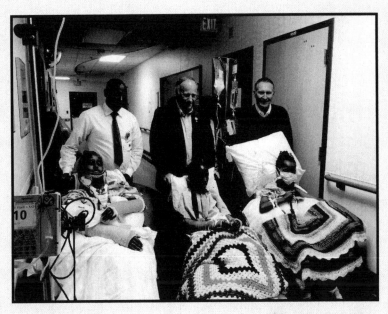

Congressman Steve King spends a Saturday morning with the children.

Press conference at Mercy Medical Center in Sioux City.

Sadhia with her boyfriends— members of the Sioux City Bandits indoor professional football team—we still kid her about these boyfriends.

Sadhia practicing throwing out the first pitch at Sioux City Explorers professional baseball game. Wilson is in the background.

Kevin and Doreen at Madonna.

Kids reunited at Ronald Mcdonald House after Doreen's discharge from Madonna.

Mamas and nurse Simphorosa praising God upon Doreen's return from Madonna.

Sadhia and Doreen at Townhouse where we had wings and fries a few times per week.

The STEMM team with Miracle Kids, mamas, Dr. Elias, and Nurse Sympharosa prior to returning to Tanzania.

A nation turns out to celebrate the kids' return and Doreen's miracle.

Home sweet home in Tanzania.

A ticker tape reception home—Tanzania style.

Lucky Vincent students welcome the Miracle Kids.

*Grief and despair
at Lucky Vincent
School remembering
the fateful day of
the crash.*

Samaritan's Purse Ed Morrow addressing the crowd at Mountainview Retreat Center at STEMM Village upon kids' return to Tanzania.

Congressman King enjoying time with children from STEMM Children's Village. He later would call that day the most significant of his life!

Dana and Dr. Steve being honored by Lucky Vincent School.

Kevin with Miracle Kids at Star Catholic High School, where all 3 now attend.

Tearful goodbyes in Tanzania.

Meyer family: Dana, Steve, Joshua, Joseph, and Elizabeth with the Miracle Kids at STEMM orphanage.

A living legend Dr. Jane visiting the Miracle Kids at STEMM Mountainview Retreat Center.

PART THREE

HOMECOMING

CHAPTER SIX

COMMUNITY HEROES

About a week after their surgeries, all the kids were sent to stay at the Ronald McDonald House in Sioux City for the duration of their recoveries. They were all doing well and were opening up to us more every day. It was a joy to watch.

Kevin says, "*Wilson healed the quickest and loved the video games. Sadhia struggled with pain more than the others and wanted chocolate cake with every meal. Doreen was sweet and positive and rarely complained, but she did have more ups and downs health-wise than the other two. She also had big back braces to handle. But I found it truly remarkable how well the kids began to recover.*"

Once Doreen started showing recovery at the Ronald McDonald House, Dr. Volz recommended she complete the remainder of her recovery at the Madonna Rehabilitation Center in Lincoln, Nebraska, for specialized spine rehab, and that Dr. Mashala go with her. At the time, she wasn't even walking yet, but after a month's stay in Lincoln, she improved tremendously.

Kevin says, "*The first time I went to visit Doreen in Lincoln, she gave me a tour of the facility with her mom and Dr. Mashala. We stopped for a snack, and then she wanted to speak with me alone. We went to a separate room, and she started begging me to keep her in Sioux City. The tears started flowing for both of us—her big alligator tears rolling down her cheeks. She knew she could not make it in her country the way she was. I told her I loved her and would do all I could to help her regain her health and be successful in her country.*

"*Her progress at Madonna was miraculous. When I visited the first time, she was using a walker, but on each successive visit, she would continue to make progress until she was discharged in August.*"

Meanwhile, Sadhia and Wilson continued to blossom at the Ronald McDonald House in Sioux City, while also winning over the hearts of Siouxland. We knew their recovery was going to be around two to three months, but we also were mindful that the kids and their mamas were far away from their comforts of home. So even though we did the best we could to keep them comfortable and feeling safe, we knew we could not send them home without nearly complete physical restoration. So we worked with them as efficiently as possible, while ensuring they made the most of their time there while healing both spiritually and emotionally.

Sadhia was in a neck collar for two months, and that was hard on her, but her personality began to shine as she settled in. In the beginning, she was angry, withdrawn, and quiet, but by the end of her stay with us, she was confident and outgoing. Such an intelligent joy to be around! And Wilson was always joyful and appreciative. Everyone gravitated toward his big smiles, and he became quite the ambassador for STEMM and for Christian goodwill.

Kevin says, "*It was such a blessing to watch the kids experience new things for the first time with such joy and amazement! There were so many firsts for them—an air dryer in a public restroom, driving my car through the church parking lot, Jolly Time popcorn, ice cream at Wells Blue Bunny, an automatic car wash, and fireworks at the baseball games. The kids told me if they had done that in Tanzania, kids would pee their pants!*

"*I spent part of most every day with them. Running to appointments, shopping, taking them to the Miracle League splash pad, movies, or just hanging out. It was a complete joy. And as they continued to heal, their personalities opened up. They each were smart, funny, and witty—unfortunately, I think my sarcasm rubbed off on them, as by the end, they could really give it to me!*

"*The staff at Ronald McDonald House was amazing. The coordinating of their schedules had to be a nightmare—they had counseling, doctor appointments, rehab, more surgery, tutoring, Bible study, dental appointments, shopping, social events, and visitors. And then you throw in 'Tanzanian time'— never ready and never in a hurry!*"

Our Miracle Kids were quite the social butterflies. They loved it all, and the community loved them! They got to flip the coin at a Bandits football game, throw out the first pitch at a Sioux City Explorers baseball game on the Fourth of July, and they were welcomed wherever they went—especially Townhouse.

Kevin says, "*We had many trips to the Townhouse, a local dive bar that served great chicken wings and French fries— an American staple for our Tanzanians! We went every week for Wing Wednesday, and sometimes more than once a week! We would eat, laugh, and learn more about each other, and it became a special place for us. The people there loved the kids. They would move chairs and tables when we'd arrive with the kids in their wheelchairs, and they would play games and win balls or stuffed animals for the kids, too. And, without a doubt, someone would always anonymously take care of the bill. When it was time to pay, the waiters would always say to me, 'It's taken care of already!' Those kids certainly impacted our community in a positive way.*"

When the kids first arrived to Sioux City, I remember we had people calling constantly, asking to bring food to them or take them out to dinner. There were more requests for some kind of involvement with the kids than I could have possibly imagined! Everyone in Siouxland wanted to be near them, and it was heartwarming to see. We were very sensitive not to turn the kids into a spectacle, but whenever they were in public, they were treated respectfully and with love.

Even though these children came to Sioux City for their own healing, it was amazing to see how they transformed the lives of others around them. From the doctors and nurses, churches and teachers, and all of us at STEMM, because of their loving nature and ability to so easily love back, they truly broke down barriers in Siouxland. They became emblematic of true love and cultural healing—things our community didn't even know they needed.

And in turn, Sioux City began to show the heart of Christianity to the world. In the context of tragedy and need, people opened up their hearts, their wallets, and their homes. They welcomed the Miracle Kids into their community and made them a forever part of their families. There was such a spirit alive that summer in Siouxland! Without any obligation, many people came forward to complete this restorative act of love and compassion, and I know that was God's will at work. I'm grateful to be part of a community who was willing to give of their time and to answer their own call in any small or mighty way.

It all made a difference.

HOMEWARD BOUND

By July, we knew it was time to start thinking about how we were going to get the kids home the following month. And we really didn't know where to start. Doreen was still in crutches and it would have been difficult for her to fly commercial. It was going to be expensive to send home eight Tanzanians! Our mission runs a very tight budget, relying on God's provision and local donations. My wife insisted I reach out to Samaritan's Purse again, but I was reluctant. They had already done so much for us! But she compelled me to at least try, so I emailed them.

Less than twenty-four hours later, they responded, "Yes, we'll take them back!" Moreover, they continued, "Also, we want to bring over medical supplies to Tanzania as well and give them to the hospitals. Thank you for letting us be a part of this story!"

Not only did Samaritan's Purse fly our kids and their mamas back home, they also packed up and sent over nineteen tons of medical equipment—over $300,000 worth!—to donate to local hospitals in Tanzania.

I was blown away by their generosity. Samaritan's Purse and particularly Reverend Franklin Graham is beyond a blessing to this story! None of this would be possible without them, and we are eternally grateful.

We planned to send the kids home on August 16, and as their departure date neared, everyone had mixed feelings. The mamas and the kids did not want to return, because they understood how different their lives had become in America and how significantly it would change when they returned home. But Kevin did a wonderful job of restoring their excitement and reminding them how good it would feel to be home again.

Kevin says, *"All the kids wanted to bring home ten bags of luggage each, but we had to explain over and over that their bags could not weigh more than 50 lbs. Apparently they had come to believe that everyone in America was nice and would let them break the rules. Ha! I had to explain to them that there were no nice Americans in an airport! Finally, we loaded up the three kids, the three mamas, Dr. Mashala, Nurse Symphorosa, as well as myself, Jennifer, Pastor Jeff of Sunnybrook, and Pastor Jon with STEMM.*

"But that was just the start! When we landed in Detroit for our flight toward Charlotte, I realized another thing the kids had never experienced before was escalators and moving side-walks! The kids laughed and laughed as they hopped on and off—but the mamas, not so much. I had to take the mamas up

the escalator one at a time, so down the escalator for me and back up again with each of them. Hilarious. When we got to Charlotte, we spent the night in a hotel before boarding our Samaritan's Purse plane the next day, and we encountered yet another new experience for them—elevators!

"*On the morning of the 17th, we went to the Samaritan's Purse hangar in Charlotte and boarded our DC-8. It was a very comfortable flight, and everyone was friendly. Doreen sat and slept by me the entire flight, and Wilson joined us now and then. As we approached Kilimanjaro International Airport, we reviewed again how we would deplane and to be positive in front of the media. The excitement grew and grew as we landed and saw all of the people waiting for the kids to arrive. What a sight!*"

Dana and I flew to Tanzania a couple days early to prepare for their arrival, because we were hosting a massive celebration at our STEMM orphanage. So when they were scheduled to land on the morning of the 18th at Kilimanjaro International Airport, we arrived early so we could greet them on the tarmac … but we weren't the only ones.

There were hundreds of thousands of Tanzanians—family, friends, fellow students and dignitaries—eagerly waiting to greet Sadhia, Wilson, and Doreen as they stepped off the plane and returned home.

CHAPTER SEVEN

THE RETURN HOME

In Tanzania, there is so much love. The people and the families give so much of their heart, and they share their emotion with reckless abandon. When they grieve, it is loud and palpable and heartfelt, but when they celebrate, their joy is magnanimous and bountiful. It feels so good to be around people of such unbridled passion. I have zero doubt in my mind that when I go to Heaven, I am going to be greeted by a chorus of Tanzanians speaking and singing in Swahili, and my motivation in life is to make that choir as big as possible.

It will be beautiful. It will be exuberant. It will be well worth the effort.

When Sadhia, Wilson, and Doreen landed in Tanzania, it was an uproar of bliss. There were thousands swarming the tarmac with flowers in hand and cheering as each deplaned. Watching Doreen walk down with her two little crutches was like witnessing a miracle! My heart flooded with the same waves of emotion I felt twenty years prior as I arrived in Tanzania myself. But this time I felt like God was acknowledging and honoring my faithfulness to him.

We did it. These kids were rescued, restored, and returned. And that's just like the story of our lives, right? We are rescued by God, restored into relationship with Him, and returned to our Heavenly Home.

It was a feeling and a moment we will never forget.

We continued to celebrate on the tarmac with speeches and a concert and cheers, and then we left for our STEMM orphanage to continue the homecoming. The ride from the airport to our orphanage is about twenty minutes, and the entire way, fellow students and locals lined the road with signs that read, "Welcome Home Miracle Kids," and, "We Love America!" Everyone was waving and cheering. What a moment for Sadhia, Wilson, and Doreen! They were all smiles.

The kids and their families spent the night at STEMM, and we gave them a tour of our orphanage in the morning. Then, we went into Arusha and visited their school, Lucky Vincent, where a a beautiful monument had been established to honor the thirty-two kids and two teachers who had died. It was an emotional visit.

Kevin says, "*The memorial was very well done, but there was so much emotion. I was concerned for the kids, as this would be the first time they would have to deal with the accident, the students who died, and the students who were at their school. We sat at a front table, with the families of the kids who died across from us. The emotion was very high, and the parents were sobbing. One father cried uncontrollably for about an hour. Then for the memorial dedication, we got wreaths of flowers to put at the memorial. The kids did great, but they were getting worn out.*"

After the school, we visited Mt. Meru Regional Hospital to visit the doctors and nurses, and then we took each of the kids home.

Kevin says, "*Doreen was first. She sat outside on a chair as the family took pictures around her, but as it came time for us to leave, she broke down. She was exhausted from the past two days, but I also believe reality set in for her, and it was my greatest fear coming to light. She was nearly hysterical, but I was able to console her.*

"*Next was Wilson, and it was like the king had returned. Neighborhood kids were there, and they swarmed him. It was a real celebration for him.*"

Lastly, we dropped off Sadhia to her uncle's house, where she would be staying. Her family was very grateful, and even though they are Muslim, they allowed Pastor Jeff to pray before we left.

After he did, the most wonderful moment happened. Sadhia has a little brother, about ten years old. And before we left, Sadhia's brother turned to Kevin and said, "I've never met Christians like you, but after being with you over the past two days, I've decided tomorrow I am going to change my religion."

The eyes of a child! All we did was live among him for two days, and he could see the face of Jesus in the people of STEMM. He saw the transformative impact of God's light shining through us, and that was enough.

That alone made everything worth it.

The following Monday, we went back to their school to set up academic plans for the kids. Remember the mock exam they were on their way to take before the accident? That actual exam was coming up in September! So we made sure the kids had proper tutoring for the test, and we discussed their start of secondary school as well. Then, Wednesday was their first day back in school, and the kids were excited.

Kevin says, "*As they entered their classroom, I noticed Sadhia grab Doreen's hand to help her in. That was a very special moment. Wilson and Doreen were noticeably closer because they lived in the same neighborhood and attended the same church. And even though Sadhia was always friendly, it was still very precious to me to watch her take Doreen's hand. Off they went."*

It was hard for Kevin to leave the kids. He committed so much of his time and heart that summer to be there for Sadhia, Wilson, and Doreen. And think of it! He was reluctant to even make the trip back in May, but now his life is forever changed, and he will love these children forever. He, Jennifer, and Manda are indeed their heroes, but there are many heroes in this story in so many ways.

By each of us answering our calls, God showed up in a BIG way. He inspired and motivated us to each find our own calling. And isn't that what this is all about? To be moved to the point of transformation? We rescued these children, restored their health and returned them home. May their story rescue you, too, restore your faith, and return your heart to your loving God.

He will call on you, and He will wait for you to answer.

CONCLUSION

As we were preparing to take the Miracle Kids to Sioux City and get them well, I had a conversation with Sadhia's dad. Sadhia was raised in a traditional Muslim home, and although her parents are divorced, her father really wanted to go to the States with us.

I remember the conversation like it was yesterday. He says to me, "I want to go, too." I tell him, "I'm sorry, sir, we need one parent to stay here and take care of the rest of your family, and Sadhia needs her mother right now." He is not convinced. I could tell he was still frustrated, so I continue, "I promise you, we fully respect your family's religion, we will take great care of your daughter, and we will be sure she can continue to practice her faith while she is away."

He stops me then and says, "I understand, but I don't know why. Why, why, why?" He pleads angrily. "*Why are you doing this?*"

He wasn't worried for his daughter's safety or well-being. He trusted us well enough. He simply did not understand our motive. So I gave him the most honest answer I want to give you today.

Why did we strive so relentlessly to take home with us three critically injured African children, and why did we give our hearts to them so abundantly? "Because the God we serve doesn't look at color or creed or country or culture. He loves all people, and he loves Sadhia and Wilson and Doreen so much that He wanted to use us as an example of Christ's love to all of Tanzania.

"He called upon us to help, and so we did."

I know this story is not easy to comprehend, but God doesn't care about the context or the result of something so much as he cares about the *intent*. What efforts do we make to abide in Him? If we are obedient to His calling, He will absolutely reward us with incredible moments and miracles and stories like this to honor our faithfulness to Him.

The Miracle Kids of Tanzania is a story that is possible only because the people in it answered their call. Then, they prayerfully and faithfully said YES. They were *willing* in so many big and small ways! And my hope for you is to embrace the truth that you, too, are an integral part of God's timeless story of mankind. You are a hero in His story, too! When all of us still our hearts and our minds—when we take ourselves out of our own menial agenda—we can begin to listen carefully for our callings. And the more time you spend with God, the more you will be able to discern His voice above all the other noise.

If you feel compelled, just begin to say yes! And believe the wonderful truth that God is a real, intimate, and loving Papa who looks after His kids and has great aspirations for us. *For you.* God is gracious and understanding, and He cares about our hearts more than you could possibly comprehend.

God is good, and this story is just a small chapter in His elaborate script and grand plan for mankind. You are a part of that plan.

Listen for His voice. Find your role. Trust your heart. Your miracle awaits. "Answer the call!"

FIRST-HAND TESTIMONIALS ABOUT THE MIRACLE KIDS

There is no way you go through an accident like this, at Karatu, and not be impacted. Despite the sadness and unimaginable death, being part of this event has been an incredible blessing. You may wonder how I can say that; but it is true, and I have felt that way since the accident.

I experienced God at a level I had never before. The timing of the events was something only He could have orchestrated. Having the people in place every step of the way was Him. Personally, I felt His arms of comfort surrounding me since the beginning. Though I searched for other reasons that my simple mind could better understand, deep down I always knew it was Him.

I saw the true goodness of humanity. My faith in humankind was strengthened. From the time of the accident through the Miracle Kids' return to Tanzania, the true human spirit was on display: compassion, sacrifice for others, doing whatever it takes, and fighting against all odds and hope was truly on display. So many people said, "YES, I will do my part," and then stepped into their "part" with passion, dedication, and excellence.

To the survivors, Doreen, Sadhia, and Wilson—the Miracle Kids. Oh, what a blessing they have been and will be for the rest of my days. They allowed a 55-year-old mzungu (white person) to remain a part of their lives.

Kevin Negaard
Executive Director – Sunnybrook Community Church

I vividly recall the early Sunday morning call I received from Steve. I hadn't heard about the tragic bus accident in Tanzania. He briefly informed me and said they had three children who needed urgent medical help. Being a pediatrician and a member of our hospital's administrative team, he reached out to ask a favor. He wanted to know if our hospital would be willing to take care of the three injured surviving children. My head began to swim. Can we really do this? This is a monumental ask! How will we get them here? Am I the right person to help take care of them? Is our hospital the right choice for them? So many questions, so few answers at that time. Without hesitation, I told Steve that, if he could get the children here, we would take care of them. Cost would not be an issue. Get them here, and we will take care of them.

The series of events over the next several days is well-documented. I remember the first time I "saw" Sadhia. She was in a CT scanner. I was looking at her images. She had multiple fractures; she was scared, isolated, and in pain. Doreen was a tiny little thing with the heart of a lion. She was the sickest, yet she rarely complained and did all we asked of her. Wilson was a trooper, the charismatic one, who always had a smile.

These children were broken in every physical and psychological way. Some bonded with their American caretakers and providers more readily than others. As I rounded on these children once, twice, sometimes three times daily, I developed a special bond with each of them. Early on things were difficult. I lost countless hours of sleep. If anything were to happen to one of the children, it could be a political nightmare, and I would never forgive myself for being partially responsible for bringing them here. They were sick and scared when they arrived, but left happy and well on their way to healing.

I'm a father of four children of my own. I am a confessed worrier. I worry about everything in my children's lives. These "adopted" children were no different. I worried most about my own abilities to take care of them. Error was not an option. I prayed, yet I still worried. As they got better, I worried less, but still prayed. I prayed not only for their physical well-being, but also for their psychological well-being. The trauma they endured during the accident, and subsequent travel half-way across the world to our community, was something no child should have to go through.

As they transitioned to the Ronald McDonald House (RMH), I began visiting them—first alone, then I introduced my family to them. We would go there to talk and share dessert. My children became their friends. My son, who is eighteen, would draw caricatures of them, tease them, essentially be the annoying big brother to them. My two youngest daughters would become their friends. To this day we stay in touch through texting.

The children and their mothers changed our lives forever. When they left, a piece of us went with them. We had a special relationship with all of them. Sadhia refers to me as her "American father." During her care, she brought me to tears on more than one occasion. That bond will never be broken.

The favor asked for on that fateful Sunday morning brought three more loving children into our lives.

Dr. Steven P. Joyce
Board Certified Internist/Pediatrician
Chief Primary Care Officer – Mercy Hospital

The story of Miracle Kids Sadhia, Wilson, and Doreen has impacted my life. On Saturday, May 5, 2017 at 10:30 a.m., I received them at Mt. Meru hospital where they were brought for treatment. I was praying for their survival all the time I took care of them. I received Sadhia Awadhi in the first ambulance at 10:30 a.m. She was in very bad shape, severely injured, unconscious, and helpless. We did whatever could be done to save her life. Wilson was smiling and very strong. He came in the second ambulance at 11:00 a.m. His smile gave me great hope that I could save their lives. The third ambulance brought Doreen at noon, who was almost gone. I had nothing to lose but to run to our ICU while holding her stretcher, resuscitate her from shock, and stabilize her. She spoke her first word when she called to me, "Uncle, I need water."

I could not close my eyes. I did whatever I could to keep them alive while waiting for help from the ministry of health, who brought the orthopedic surgeon from Muhimbili National Hospital in Dar es Salaam.

I was filled with hope when Dr. Steve Meyer read the kid's x-rays and said: "They can be treated in the U.S." I was not sure if I had heard him correctly, but I felt like a great burden was taken from my heart and a great help had come to my hand. I was sure that the kids would survive.

I was appointed to accompany the kids with their mamas to the U.S. for the treatment. I brought anointing water onto the plane and sprayed the kids. During all twenty hours of the flight, I prayed to Almighty God and Jesus Christ to let us arrive safely in Iowa. That was the most difficult mission of my entire life.

My stay at Sioux City was smooth, with much help from friends. I completed my mission of saving the lives of the kids on August 18, 2017. When I met Dr. Steve at Kilimanjaro International Airport, he hugged me and said, "Hello, my dear brother. It's done." I was almost crying with joy to see the kids getting out of the DC-8 with good health, happy and smiling to everyone. Glory to God who gave life back to our Miracle Kids.

Through this story I learned three things:

1) God's ways and thoughts are not the same as humans'. He can save His people in such an unusual way that everyone will be surprised.

2) Regardless of professionalism, expertise, and intellect, faith in Jesus Christ will always add on qualities of what we are always doing and make us to be different from one another and save and lead us through unbelievable situations.

3) Without God I am nothing, but with Him I am safe and strong.

Both my family and I have surrendered to Jesus, and we see him daily in whatever we are doing. He shows us where we belong.

Dr. Elias Mashala
Chief Orthopedic Surgeon – Mt. Meru Hospital
Arusha, Tanzania

Last summer, my world changed in a way I never would have imagined. I am a teacher and I was expecting a summer of rest and relaxation. I'd had a rough last quarter of school and was even considering a career change. This was particularly troubling to me, as I've known my whole life I was called to teach.

I heard about the Miracle Children through my good friend Kevin Negaard. He was one of the first people on the site of the bus accident in Tanzania who helped with triage.

Because he's a member of my small group at church, he shared a lot about the whole situation. My heart was broken for these families.

I wanted to reach out any way I could when I heard the children would be receiving their medical care in Sioux City. Kevin suggested I tutor the children once they were feeling well enough. I couldn't imagine these children sitting through tutoring sessions in their conditions, but I was certainly going to make myself available.

What I thought was going to be a few hours of tutoring a week, turned into so much more! First of all, I'd never worked with anyone, let alone three children, who had overcome such physical and emotional pain. Sadhia, Wilson, and Doreen are three of the strongest people I have ever met. Even in their pain, they wanted to learn and make the most of their situation, which included days of physical therapy and doctor's appointments. Their resilience was inspiring, to say the least.

In addition to working with the children, I came to know their mamas very well. I'm not much of a shopper, but I had the joy of introducing them to Walmart and HyVee. They couldn't get enough of our culture. During one trip to Walmart, a woman approached us and said she'd heard about their story on TV and was wanting to meet them. She was from Congo and her fiancé was from Tanzania. She invited all of us to their upcoming wedding!

Over the summer, I met many native Africans who live in the Siouxland area and learned about their personal stories. I got to learn more about students from my own school and how their families moved to South Dakota from Africa. I can speak enough Swahili to be dangerous (Google Translate was the most-used app on my phone during this time). My world got so much bigger. Issues in my life felt like nothing in comparison to the stories of these families. Daily, I counted my blessings.

These children and mamas not only renewed my love for teaching; they became my extended family. I never thought of traveling overseas, but I am making plans to travel with STEMM in August of 2018. Besides my husband and children, I communicate with at least one of the families almost daily through text. I was, and am, so blessed to be a part of this story. I'm looking forward to following them as they grow and hopefully return to the States for college. I am so glad I could be part of the hands and feet of God for these families. Part of my heart will always be in Tanzania.

Lora Meyers
Teacher

When we first heard about the tragedy in Tanzania and the potential transfer of the children to Mercy Medical Center for definitive care, I was in a board room with our leadership team. We seemed to share the same emotions—how tragic for these children. These families, are they really going to come here? Are we able to care for these severely injured children? Are we the right facility for this? Should they go to a dedicated children's hospital? These concerns were quickly washed away by the realization that these children were in dire need, and we were given the opportunity to transform their lives and would do everything possible to ensure we did that.

Trying to anticipate the many medical, social, and emotional needs of these children and their families was initially overwhelming. Over the next several hours it became evident that this would be an opportunity for the whole hospital community to refocus on what we do best—care for others in need. As word spread through the community about the events in Tanzania, phone calls and donations from volunteers, nurses, surgical vendors and physicians poured in. It took less than two minutes of phone calls to assemble the team of physicians to provide the free care from orthopedic surgeons, neurosurgeons, oral maxillofacial, trauma, anesthesia, and pediatrics.

The memory of standing on the tarmac at the Sioux City airport, awaiting the medical transport flight to land, and praying for God's hand to support my team, these children, and their families through their recovery will remain with me forever. Full of anxiety, I stood calmly watching the plane land as the children were unloaded from the aircraft after days of travel, seeing their broken bodies, their terrified and exhausted eyes.

Over the following days, weeks, and months the children slowly improved and prepared to return to Tanzania. Their recovery represented the healing and impact they had on me and our staff. Numerous caregivers thanked us for the opportunity to help the children. This confirmed that the children had a much larger impact on us than we had on them.

As surgeons and hospital administrators, we have the opportunity to be with people at some of the most difficult times of their lives—and hopefully be able to make an impact. Those events are what drive us to do what we do. The challenging patients and families, the long hours and late nights, the personal events you had to miss—all that is washed away by the moments where we can care for those in need. The weeks and months of my life touched by Doreen, Sadhia, Wilson, their families, and the care team from Tanzania restored my belief that keeping God's mission to care for those in need at the center of each decision I make ensures that we will always make it right.

Lawrence Volz, M.D.
General Surgeon, Midlands Clinic Chief Medical Officer –
Mercy Hospital

On Monday, May 8, 2017, I was traveling on a Congressional Delegation fact finding trip through Greece, Italy, and the Balkans. While I was at an event hosted by the U.S. Embassy in Athens, engaged in an intense conversation, my cell phone rang. I drew my phone expecting to decline the call. My screen read "Steve Meyer." Dr. Meyer is a hunting buddy, a surgeon, and a missionary. He never calls for something frivolous, so I answered immediately, half expecting a request for a minor miracle.

Dr. Meyer said, "You have heard about the awful bus wreck in Tanzania." I hadn't, and he filled me in on the awful tragedy that killed thirty-five of thirty-eight bus passengers on a dangerous road near Arusha, Tanzania. He said, "I can't save them here in Tanzania. We have to fly them back to Sioux City where we have the necessary medical equipment and a team of volunteers ready. Everything is set up to take care of them. Steve, I need you to expedite the passports and visas, and to find a medevac plane that can fly three severely critical kids, their mothers, and a doctor and nurse to Iowa. They won't live much longer unless we can get them to Mercy Hospital in Sioux City." This was going to take more than a minor miracle.

I immediately employed some of the U.S. Embassy staff to chase down phone numbers and help make phone connections. My first effective call was to the U.S. Embassy in Tanzania where I spoke with Anthony Pagliai, the Counsel General. Mr. Pagliai could expedite the visas if Tanzanian passports could be processed in time. Dr. Meyer had already employed the services of Lazaro Nyalandu, a Minister in the Tanzanian government and mutual friend. Mr. Pagliai knew of Lazaro, which gave our requests more credibility. Lazaro was key to getting the passports expedited for all eight who would make the trip. Mr. Pagliai expedited the visas. The easiest part was in motion.

Adding to the challenge were the logistical complications for me because I was soon back in the air on the way to Sarajevo. I had been making calls in search of a medevac plane. I began calling every source I could think of, including the White House. I was encouraged by the responses that I received from the Trump team but I couldn't get a "yes." In Bosnia, I employed the Embassy personnel again in search of a plane. Steve Meyer called me again to check on any progress and, I think, to give me a greater sense of urgency along with his update. Still, the toughest link to form in the chain of miracles Meyer was forging for the future "Miracle Kids" was to get a plane. U.S. assets in that part of the world are thin and it is necessary that we hold our military assets close to our troops to protect them. I received a return call from the White House and was asked, "Are the survivors U.S. citizens?" At that moment, I knew we wouldn't get a military plane. It was a big disappointment but I was glad I had other lines in the water.

We then flew to Albania, arriving late. Some of us planned a strategy that evening and I took up the search for a plane the next morning. Again, the U.S. Embassy stepped up to help. By early afternoon, we had set up a call with Reverend Franklin Graham of Samaritan's Purse and the stellar son of the late Reverend Billy Graham. I called Franklin at 4:00 p.m. Albanian time. He answered the call immediately and listened as I made my, by now, practiced pitch for a medevac plane. In little more than three minutes, Graham said, "We have a DC-8 that can be set up for them and we'll fly the children and their supporting personnel to Iowa for you." There it was! This was the "yes" I had been working for. I had found a plane on the tarmac in the Mid-East but the cost was $300,000. With that in mind, I said, "Thank you, Reverend Graham, but I don't know that I can raise the money." Graham said without hesitation, "You won't need to. We will take care of it for you." His words confirmed that the chain of miracle was coming together. I said to Graham, "I will text you Dr. Meyer's cell and yours to him with a message to immediately call each other." Now the two of them would need to connect and work out the logistics. I was on the way to the airport again on the "country-a-day tour" to Macedonia, then Kosovo, then Italy. I was in Kosovo when I learned that Reverend Graham and Dr. Meyer had connected and that the DC-8 would soon arrive in Tanzania to pick up the "Miracle Kids" and fly them to Sioux City. My count was that I had worked with six U.S. Embassies just to forge my single link in the Meyer chain of God's miracles necessary to save the lives of the kids.

Upon my return to Iowa, I couldn't wait to get to Mercy Medical Center to see the kids. It was an utter joy to see their faces and the light in their eyes. Little more than a week earlier they had been at death's door. Their mothers by now understood their children were going to pull through. Even with the language barrier, they left no doubt about their gratitude. The worst remaining news was that Doreen was paralyzed from the waist down.

Two weeks later, I receive another call from Steve. He said, "I'm calling to tell you about another miracle. I went in to check on Doreen and teased her as I usually do, and she kicked me! Neurologists won't agree with me, but she will walk again!" At that point we began planning the return of the "Miracle Kids" to their home country. We set August 18 as the date and I began planning to be there to welcome them home.

The best place in the world to be on August 18 was on the tarmac at Kilimanjaro Airport to welcome the "Miracle Kids" home. Led by Lazaro Nyalandu, my wife, Marilyn and I, along with Steve and Dana Meyer shared in the utter elation of a nation as we celebrated the joy of our homecoming together. The highest of many high points was when Doreen walked down the steps of the ramp from the Samaritan's Purse DC-8 on her own and set foot on her home country. That was the moment of the greatest cheer from thousands of Tanzanians, who were dressed in their Sunday best for the occasion.

The program included the Tanzanian national anthem followed by "The Star-Spangled Banner." Thousands stood proudly and sang on key in Swahili at the top of their lungs. We Americans would be next and we were only four. I leaned over to Dr. Meyer and said, "We are really going to have to belt this one out." He agreed, and we really delivered! I had never sung our national anthem with such pride as we celebrated the joy of serving God and America.

Steve asked me to say a few words at the annual STEMM auction in the fall. I only said that it is rare to have the opportunity to forge just one link in a chain of miracles that saves lives. I was only one link. Dr. Meyer put the links together and was the linchpin of the entire life-saving effort. Reverend Franklin Graham was a timely and essential link as well. We can't forget Kevin, Manda, and Jennifer, the STEMM volunteers who pulled the children out of the bus and who have been with them every step of the way. Scores of lives were changed by this tragedy. Given the gruesome scope of the loss of life and the injuries, the best possible outcome has been realized. There is now a bright future as a result of the chain of miracles, shaped through His servants by the hand of God.

Steve King
14-year Congressman – Iowa 4th District

Although it has been almost a year, I clearly remember looking at my cell phone as the display on the mobile device signaled an incoming call from Tanzania. Since I don't generally receive calls from eastern Africa, I assumed this was something like the e-mail scams promising money from the estate of a deceased multi-millionaire. I decided not to answer.

A moment later, my phone rang again. This time, the caller ID showed that Dr. Steve Meyer, a local orthopedic surgeon, was trying to reach me. I quickly connected the dots, as Steve is known for his medical missions and philanthropic work in Tanzania. I immediately answered the phone.

Dr. Meyer expeditiously explained that he was soliciting assistance to bring three young Tanzanian children to the United States to receive life-saving medical care in the wake of a tragic bus crash that had claimed the lives of thirty-three children and three adults on the other side of the world. He stated that he had already reached our congressman and he was hoping that I would contact our United States Senators.

Steve became a tireless advocate for the children. Through his sheer willpower and a steadfast refusal to take "no" for an answer, he found a way to transport the survivors to the United States. Hours later, the children were in emergency surgery at Mercy Medical Center in Sioux City, Iowa. Within a day or two, I attended a press conference in the hospital lobby where Dr. Meyer and a team of physicians confirmed that the children were stable, would require multiple surgeries, months of high-level medical care, including physical therapy, and that all of it would be covered free of charge.

As media around the world reported this breaking international news, the three medical missionaries who happened upon that horrific bus crash, and provided the initial triage at the scene, began to tell their incredible story. Notably, the rescuers were joined in Iowa by representatives of the Tanzanian government and the mothers of the three surviving children who repeatedly thanked all involved for bringing their children to the United States and saving their lives.

Dr. Meyer's remarkable story of the rescue, transport, and improbable medical recovery of the Tanzanian "Miracle Kids" is a testament to individual determination and, ultimately, a tribute to human compassion. Perhaps most importantly, it is also a timeless reminder that, regardless of country, color, or creed, we are all God's children.

Chris McGowan

President, Siouxland Chamber of Commerce

The Miracle Kids Story is a Relational Masterpiece, created and played out as only the only true "Master of Relationships," who is God Himself, could! How else could people and events spanning nearly 40 years and 2 continents, suddenly and supernaturally be brought together, as though all responding to one call, to powerfully affect the destinies; first, of 3 critically ill children, and then, those of countless others in their wake?

No One but God could do this!

- A young seminarian, in 1980, seeking to serve God with his wife on the mission field
- A doctor, 16 years later, whose life has fallen apart after an affair and bitter divorce

- A young and extremely poor Tanzanian student, studying at a Junior College in Iowa, with a dream to help other struggling students in his nation to receive an education and escape poverty
- A surprising visit with the First Lady of Tanzania and a friend of hers, who would become the Vice President of the nation 20 years later

These are only a few of the dots connected, along with the following.

- Three very unsuspecting individuals who, though unknown to each other, came together to help with medical outreach in a faraway land
- A politician
- An entire hospital in Iowa
- A mercy ministry in North Carolina

All of these people and entities were brought together—supernaturally—at one moment in time, to intervene in a national catastrophe and bring healing and restoration to three desperately ill students. This never should have happened. This should have been an absolute impossibility. And yet, when God steps in, and people say, "Yes," anything can happen! And it did happen—all to the glory of God!

Read the story. You will be amazed. Yes, our God is that good! He can use anyone and everyone in His unfolding

Miracle Story. Will you trust Him? Will you say "Yes" when He calls on you?

Jon Gerdts

the "young seminarian," now pastor of 35 years
Executive Director of STEMM

The first night Kevin Negaard phoned me to ask if he could reserve a table for the himself and the children from Tanzania that traveled back to the US for medical treatment for injuries suffered in a bus accident, I didn't think much of it. Then the next week he phoned again with the same request... Kevin has been a good customer and an even better friend for many years, so again, I didn't put much thought into it the request. This became a routine over the next several weeks.

One of these nights I stopped at Kevin's table and the children were all eating Buffalo wings and french fries with some relatives. They were all smiles and said "hi" while eating. Kevin expressed his thanks for the hospitality and the generosity we were showing his new friends. That comment caught me off guard a little, as I thought to myself, *'that's what we are here for, to serve people.'* It was then that Kevin informed me that our customers, usually anonymously, were picking up their table's tab many of the nights they came in to eat. I'm sure the smile on my face stayed intact for several days.

I always knew we had some of the best customers in the area, but this outpouring of support for a group of children they didn't know from Adam reaffirmed that feeling. Kevin also informed me the children asked all the time if they could go back for wings and fries. So again, I have always said the Townhouse has the best wings in the area, but now I could say they were the best in the World—at least in their world. To know that something we take for granted every day gave these children such joy made me feel even better about what we do each and every day.

We look forward to hosting the children when they return to Sioux City. They will always have a special place in our hearts.

Rick Dominowski

Owner/Manager – Townhouse Restaurant
Sioux City, IA

Keeping families together at the toughest of times. That's the mission and purpose of the Ronald McDonald House Charities (RMHC) of Siouxland. So it felt very fitting that we would get the call to help in this situation.

The first call came from Samaritan's Purse just a few days after the bus crash in Tanzania. RMHC of Siouxland staff had already been discussing the role we could play if, in fact, the children were brought to Sioux City for treatment. So the answer to the question 'Can you help?' was 'Most definitely, yes.' RMHC of Siouxland was the only place the families could stay for an extended period of time and be together. With the vast cultural differences the families would be faced with in Sioux City, staying together in one place seemed like the best way to ensure a community feeling of togetherness and support while the children healed.

It wasn't long after that when Steve and Dana Meyer came for a visit. They were still unsure the role RMHC would play, but happy to see what could be offered. A week later, Dana returned with the three Tanzanian mothers and a nurse to tour our house. From the moment they walked through the door, the Tanzanian families called our house a home for 12 weeks. In those weeks, our staff did all they could to make the families comfortable in our home, but the community also stepped up to make sure our house had all it needed and more for the families.

I remember not long after the families came to stay with us hearing someone say 'Your house will never be the same again.' They were right. In so many ways, allowing Wilson, Sahdia, Doreen and their families to stay with us changed each one of us. Over 12 weeks, we made daily trips to the hospital for therapy, taught them to use American appliances, shared meals and built friendships. Our house was the center of their daily lives where they took English lessons, had Bible study, did their schooling and cooked their meals. We shared cultural traditions, many struggles and victories, sadness and celebrations, and we witnessed three children in wheelchairs begin to walk, run, and smile again.

At RMHC of Siouxland, we know that children endure tough medical situations much better when surrounded by those they love. When families stay with us they receive food to eat and a place to sleep. But what we feel is the most important is the intangible gifts this community resource provides by allowing families to be together; the gift of hugs; the gift of giggles; the gift of smiles; and most importantly the gift of togetherness. That's why we know the role we were called to play in the recovery of Wilson, Sahdia and Doreen was critical. What a blessing to play that role. What a blessing to witness three children in visible pain and sadness recover and return to their home country walking again with smiles on their faces.

We are proud to have taken the call to help the Tanzanian families in May of 2017. We are proud of the role the community helped us play in their lives. And we are proud to call each one of them our family.

Christy Batien
Executive Director – RHMC of Siouxland

From the beginning of the story of the Tanzanian Children who survived the horrific bus crash, people have ascribed the term "miracle" to the fact of their survival. If the world would take the time to read the details of this account of their story it would be obvious that their survival was only the first of many miracles and God moments. The Christian reader will be amazed and their faith would be strengthened by the accounts of how God showed up and orchestrated the kids' survival, healing, and return home. The agnostic reader will be challenged to explain Doreen, Sadhia, and Wilson's experiences by attributing it only to coincidence or altruism of generous people.

As I look back over the accounts of Tanzanian Miracle Kids I am struck by a single fact, a single experience that was made up by multiple miracles and multiple supernatural interventions. From the outside looking in the story may be inspiring and interesting, but as one who was involved in the details of the transport and initial care of the children I can personally attest to the fact that their story is one characterized by many smaller but important and critically timed God interventions.

In the Old Testament, followers of God would often build an altar of stones at the place where they experienced a miracle from God. One reason they did this was to ensure that those who followed them were reminded of God's miracles and His faithfulness. This book, like the altars of remembrance in the

Old Testament, is important in the fact it is an intentional effort to document God's miracles and his daily workings in our lives. His interventions in our lives are sometimes very visible and large, such as when He saves three very special children from a bus crash that killed all of their schoolmates. Other times He shows up in the small ways by having orchestrated a Samaritan's Purse staff who spoke Swahili to be in the region and who was able to care for and minister to the children as they travelled to the US from Tanzania on the Samaritan's Purse DC-8.

My experience in working with Doreen, Sadhia, and Wilson is an experience of God's faithfulness and his detailed intervention, provision, and care for all of His creation in the small details of our lives. Large miracles like the children surviving the bus crash are easy to see. The smaller miracles such as STEMM volunteers just happening to be on the same road as the bus crash at the same time, or the fact that Samaritan's Purse had a staff in the region who spoke the local language, or that the Samaritan's Purse DC-8 had an opening in its normally packed schedule, are some of the many examples of how God worked in the small details, some even months in advance, to make sure that Sadhia, Doreen, and Wilson were cared for at the moment they needed it most.

Drew Privette

Deputy Director/ International Projects – Samaritan's Purse

How does one articulate the indescribable? There are no words to accurately capture the splendor of Kilimanjaro or the vast magnificence of the Serengeti. In like manner I find it challenging to describe the surreal events and transformative impact of this epic story on my life.

Being in the maelstrom of an evolving miracle is beyond humbling. There is absolutely nothing special or unique about me! To be utilized by God in this epic narrative still feels unbelievable. Yet in this story I have tasted so much of the goodness of God, my friend. I have seen so much of the loving hearts of His most precious creation—my fellow believers—that I feel as though I have been blessed to stand on "Holy Ground".

This most certainly is not a testimony to me or any persons or even a cool story to tell. This book is a faithful response to God's command to tell future generations of his miracles. Psalm 78 specifically states that if we tell future generations of God's miracles they will love Him and obey His commands.

As I write this I am still overwhelmed by the loving, caring hearts of my community of Siouxland. In a predominantly white Midwest paragon of blue-collar America, I witnessed true, unconditional love for three black African children. During this unparalleled time of divisiveness in our country and the world at large, the human spirit of love and compassion exemplified by our community toward three strangers of different color, culture and creed fills me with hope for the future of mankind. I pray it does the same for you!

This epic tale has compelled our ministry (STEMM) to embrace an entirely new mindset. We are now committed to always be "Spirit led–relationally driven." Only the Holy Spirit could compel so many hearts to answer God's call. Only God could orchestrate so many relationships over decades of time to accomplish The Impossible.

This story has shown me beyond a doubt that God is good—better than we can ever imagine! God has a plan for every individual's life. We have access to a mighty God's infinite and indeterminable power if we enter into His story. Through this story, it is now indisputable to me that miracles—large and small—occur each and every day, orchestrated by God through His people. With God all things are possible when we ANSWER HIS CALL.

Dr. Steve Meyer
Orthopedic Surgeon – CNOS
Founder STEMM

ABOUT THE AUTHOR

D r. Steve Meyer is a fellowship-trained (pediatric) orthopedic surgeon at CNOS in Dakota Dunes, South Dakota. He was also co-founder and, for the past twenty years, president of Siouxland Tanzania Educational Medical Ministry (STEMM). His love for his practice in orthopedics and for his patients is beyond evident. His true passion, however, is impacting lives on both sides of the ocean for God's Kingdom through the STEMM ministry.

His lovely wife, Dana, and their six collective beautiful children are his number-one priority. Athletic and outdoor activities of all sorts (gardening, hunting, fishing, etc.) fill what little free-time remains. Dr. Steve lives in Sioux City, Iowa with his family in the home he and Dana were married in over twenty years ago, and is an active member of Sunnybrook Church.

ABOUT THE COMPANY

The Siouxland Tanzania Educational Medical Ministry (STEMM) is a 501(c)3 non-profit chartered in 1997 to address the dire needs of the people, particularly the children, of Tanzania. Its secondary goal is to provide an avenue for mission trips with STEMM to Tanzania. Their stated mission is to change lives for Christ through compassionate care and their vision is to develop Tanzania into a vibrant, Christian community. Current areas of endeavor include educational support and mentorship, medical outreach, orphan care, school feeding programs, agricultural empowerment, and community development. We welcome individuals, churches, and organizations to experience mission through a STEMM trip to Tanzania. STEMM is compelled to remain "Spirit-led and relationally driven."

Website: www.stemm.org
Office: 712-258-8282
Email: office@stemm.org
Facebook: facebook.com/STEMM1996
Address: 505 5th Street Suite 206
Sioux City, IA 51102